THE TALES OF HELEN AND LYSANDER - A SPARTAN GIRL AND BOY

The Trials of Training

Stephen Hodgson

Tim Saunders Publications

TS

Tim Saunders Publications

Copyright © 2024 Stephen Hodgson

All rights reserved

This book is a work of fiction which includes some references to historical characters and events.

No part of this book may be reproduced, or stored in a retrieval system, or transmitted in any form or by any means, electronic, mechanical, photocopying, recording, or otherwise, without express written permission of the publisher.

To read more about Helen and Lysander please go to: www.helenandlysander.com

Cover illustration by Sophie Hunter

"A city is well fortified that has a wall of men instead of brick."

LYCURGUS OF SPARTA

CONTENTS

Title Page	
Copyright	
Epigraph	
Foreword	
Book 1	1
Prologue	2
Chapter I	5
Chapter II	46
Chapter III	84
Chapter IV	127
Chapter V	177
Chapter VI	224
Chapter VII	243
Chapter VIII	248
Chapter IX	250
Chapter X	254
Chapter XI	258
Chapter XII	266
Chapter XIII	271
Chapter XIV	277

Chapter XV	285
Chapter XVI	289
Chapter XVII	295
Chapter XVIII	302
Acknowledgements	309
Also from Tim Saunders Publications	310
About The Author	311

FOREWORD

Welcome to this first in a series of books I intend to write about growing up in ancient Sparta. I have tried to create a world as close as I can to how it might have felt, smelt, looked and sounded to live in the ancient city state of Sparta in and around the start of the fifth century BC. The world I have created is, I believe, a compelling one and I have tried to make it as accurate as possible within the confines of telling a story. This is, above all, a work of fiction based in a historical setting rather than a history.

I hope you will enjoy entering the lives of my characters: Helen, Lysander and Pylos as much as I have enjoyed creating them. I hope that you will find the story of their entry into the *agoge* - the famed Spartan training academy - an absorbing and thrilling one.

My inspiration for writing this series of books stems from two sources. Firstly, my love of history and the ancient world - we really owe them so much. Secondly, my love of reading - both by myself and with my two boys as they were growing up. I wrote this story with them in mind and happy memories of many hours spent reading books together. I hope you will enjoy entering this world, too.

BOOK 1

The Trials of Training

PROLOGUE

Lysander's fist smacked into the back of the tall boy's head. There was a loud crack as the bones in Lysander's hand protested at being used for such a blow. Lysander acted out of impulse. The boy he hit was choking his friend. He hadn't really appreciated just how hard the back of someone's head could be and he hadn't formed a proper fist. He was sure that he had broken the bones in his hand. The punch had the desired effect though. His friend was no longer being strangled. Instead, the attention was now all on Lysander.

Lysander was expecting to get punched in the face by the tall boy but, before he knew what was happening, he was grabbed from behind by two other boys, quickly pinned to the floor and hit a few times for good measure. The tall boy stopped and looked around him to survey the scene. He looked at the small boy whose nose he had just broken and from which blood was pouring like water from a tap. He looked at the fair-haired boy he had just been strangling, who had a bright red face and was coughing. And he looked at Lysander, who had punched him but who was now restrained on the floor. The tall boy shouted menacingly, "Anybody else want to challenge me?"

There were no takers. This boy was now the leader of Lysander's new pack.

At roughly the same time that this was happening, Helen, Lysander's twin sister, was also experiencing a shock. She had just spent the evening with her family, being given gifts by her father. Now she was faced with **this**...

This was an older, very fierce looking woman standing at her doorstep telling her, "I don't like you… I don't want to be here… I'm going to make you pay for this."

Helen didn't understand. Her mother had told her last night that this woman was the best trainer in the whole of Sparta and that she had agreed to train Helen as a favour to her mother. She had trained her mother who said that she loved her and was looking forward to training Helen.

This very clearly was not the case. The old woman continued, "Well, are you going to invite me in, you stupid girl? Or are you just going to stand there like an idiot with your mouth wide open?"

Both Lysander and Helen couldn't quite understand what was happening.

It was only last night that they had both had the most wonderful feast with their parents and had spent a fantastic evening together in a lovely, warm family environment.

Just one night later, they had been thrown into very different worlds.

And neither of them liked it.

To help them understand how they had got here, the thoughts of both of them turned independently to the events of yesterday.

CHAPTER I
Yesterday (the feast)

I

Lysander jumped as the plate crashed onto the floor and shattered into small pieces. Cakes covered in honey and pine nuts scattered everywhere.

The *helot* boy, Pylos, looked horrified as the plate had slipped from his hands. Lysander's mother, Demetria, looked both shocked and angry at the same time. She shouted at Pylos, "You stupid *helot*! Get a broom and clear up that mess now! ...And get your mother to put more cakes in the oven."

Pylos hated that word, "*helot*". It denoted everything that was bad about his and his mother's life. It described their position in Spartan society - at the very bottom - and it set out his future for him - a life of slavery with no escape. He hated it but he could not challenge it. So, he just stared at the floor in a mixture of anger and shame.

Then, as an afterthought, Demetria added, "You'll pay for this from your own food ration, you clumsy boy!

Demetria was clearly agitated. Her emotions were high because today was a very special day

- probably the most special day that any Spartan household could experience. It was Lysander's last day living with his family. Tomorrow he would join the *agoge*, the famed Spartan training academy which, from the age of seven and over the next eleven years, would turn him into a warrior. So, Demetria was sad because she would be saying goodbye to her son forever after tonight. But she was also proud because this was the highest honour a mother could give to Sparta. To produce a fine, strong boy and send him off to join the *agoge* was the single most useful thing a mother could do to help ensure the survival of Sparta. It was her contribution to Sparta's future and it meant that she would be able to live out the rest of her days as the proud mother of a fabled warrior. She looked forward to walking around Sparta with her head held high and hearing the other women whisper as she passed, *"That's Demetria, the mother of Lysander, the famous warrior."*

So, today Demetria wanted everything to be perfect. She turned to Pylos again and spoke to him angrily. "All you and your mother, Lampita, have to do is take care of the cooking and cleaning and tend to the vegetables in the garden. It's not exactly hard work, is it? It's not like training to be a warrior. You *helots* are so ungrateful! We give you a home, we feed you, we keep you under our roof and we keep you safe. In return, we only ask you to keep the household running. It's not too much to ask, is it? You stupid, clumsy boy!"

Lampita could see that Demetria was getting more and more angry. Her face was getting red and her words were coming out faster and faster. Lampita decided that she needed to calm the situation. "I am so sorry, Mistress Demetria," she said. "I will bake some more cakes straight away. I will add some extra honey to them so that they are even more delicious than the ones Pylos has spoiled. I know how important tonight is to you and Lysander. I will make sure that Pylos and I prepare you the best feast ever. Please don't punish Pylos, he is just a stupid boy and I will teach him how to do it better next time." Demetria breathed out deeply and the colour from her cheeks started to drain away.

It was clear that Lampita's words had worked but Demetria still felt she had to spell things out clearly one more time. "Just see that you do, Lampita," she said. "Tonight is Lysander's passing out feast. His father, Leon, will come home and join the celebration. We see Leon so rarely. I want everything to be just right for both of them. I want everything to be perfect. I want to give them a feast fit for the two Kings of Sparta."

"Yes, Mistress Demetria," Lampita replied, looking at the floor in shame. "I understand. We will not let you down again."

II

But Lysander was not the only person whose celebration it was that day. His twin sister, Helen, was also coming of age.

"What about me, Mother?" she said. "Isn't it my special day, too?"

Helen knew the answer. She was not joining the *agoge* - that was just for boys - but she would be entering her own training programme at home and in the *gymnasium*. So, her life was going to be different too and she resented the fact that her mother was only speaking about Lysander. She asked the question to make the point that Lysander always got special treatment in the family just because he was a boy.

"Of course, darling," replied Demetria. "I've told you this already. You will be trained in sports, hunting, the arts and the law. In that way, you will grow up to be fit and strong, able to feed your family, sing and dance at festivals and help to govern Sparta. Sparta is the finest city in all of Greece and you will learn to play your part in its future too."

When her mother started talking about how great Sparta was, Helen knew from experience that her mother would be talking for a long time. She realised that her mother was talking too much out of embarrassment for speaking to Lampita only about Lysander.

Helen decided to try to cut her mother short and to lighten the mood in the house. She decided to make a joke out of Pylos's mistake and to make her own point about Lysander's favourable treatment again.

"Those broken cakes are good enough for Lysander," she said. "The freshly baked ones will be mine. After all, Spartan women always come second to Spartan men - so it's only right that I get the second lot of cakes!"

Unfortunately, Helen's joke had the opposite effect. It caused her mother to get angry and to talk about Sparta even more.

"Shush, Helen," snapped Demetria. "Don't say such ridiculous things. You know you are lucky to live in Sparta. How many times have we spoken about this? Sparta gives its women more rights than any other city in the whole of Greece. Thank your lucky stars that you were not born in Athens. If you had been born Athenian you would learn to cook and clean like a *helot* and you would be expected only to make babies."

Helen fell silent. She knew her mother was right and she realised that humour wasn't going to work in these circumstances. She still felt that Spartan men and boys did have the best of the deal and that it was unfair. She was jealous of Lysander and the fact that he was to join the *agoge*. He would grow up to be famous. He would fight for Sparta and his name would be mentioned in songs and poems for years to come.

III

Meanwhile, Lysander was busy helping to clean up the cakes. He was on his hands and knees picking up the broken or dirty cakes and putting them into a bag to give to the animals later. But he kept the small number of cakes that were still clean and unbroken and put them into another bag. He said to Pylos under his breath, "These are for you and Lampita. I don't want you both to go hungry on my account. I'll put them under my cloak and you can take them later."

Pylos had tears in his eyes but he gave a little smile to Lysander in return for his kindness. He had expected to be beaten or worse for his mistake and so he was relieved to get away with only a food punishment. The fact that Lysander had helped him with that punishment made him feel even more grateful to Lysander.

This was not the only time that Lysander had been kind to Pylos.

Lysander knew that every Spartan household had to have slaves or *helots* so that the Spartans could concentrate on running Sparta but he felt sorry for Pylos and his mother. Pylos was about his own age and he thought that he and Pylos could have been friends if his ancestors hadn't been captured by the Spartans many years ago and if Pylos had not been made a *helot.*

Just at that point Demetria spotted what was happening and she shouted angrily at Lysander, "Lysander, what are you doing? Stand up at once and leave that to Pylos! You know that friendly relations are not permitted between *helots* and Spartans."

She grabbed him by the hand and took him to the corner of the room. She kneeled down so that her face was at the same level as his own. She spoke directly to him and wagged her finger in his face.

"I have spoken to you about this before. Now that you are about to enter the *agoge* you cannot be seen to be friendly to a *helot*. Even to Pylos. If you are seen helping or being friendly to a *helot* when you are outside this house you will be punished by the *ephors*. In front of everyone in Sparta. The *ephors* will punish you without mercy and they will kill the *helot*. You must not do it. Do you understand?"

Lysander looked down at his feet and nodded his head to signal to his mother that he understood. He hated this rule. His mother had not strictly enforced it in the house when he was young but now he was leaving he understood that he would be punished if caught and that Pylos would have an even worse fate. So, Lysander decided in future to help Pylos only where he could without being seen.

IV

Demetria was very upset with the way that things were going. She had hoped to get everything perfect for the feast and yet here they all were - arguing and shouting and breaking things. As the woman of the house she realised that it was her responsibility to get things back on track. She stood up after speaking to Lysander and clapped her hands loudly to get everyone's attention. "Everyone, we have only a few hours before Leon will return from the common mess. Let's take stock of the preparations for tonight. This has to be a feast for everyone to remember."

"Why does Father come home so rarely?" asked Helen. "Does he not like us?"

This was a question that Helen didn't know the answer to. Her father came to the house sometimes but only briefly. He never ate with them and he never slept in the house. She had always wondered why this was the case. She had asked her mother a few times but she had never really got a clear reply.

"Stupid girl," hissed Demetria. "Don't say such things. You know as well as I do that it's the rules. I've told you before. Spartan men are not allowed to eat or live at home until they are thirty years old. Men under thirty always eat and sleep in their common mess."

Lysander's ears pricked up. He had heard of

the common mess and he knew that this was where he would eat after tonight but he didn't really know much about it. This seemed a good point to ask. It would also distract his mother from being angry with Helen.

"What's the common mess?" he asked.

"It is the group of soldiers you will train with and grow up with in the *agoge*," Demetria replied, slightly wearily. "The bond you will form with them will last for the rest of your lives and will make you loyal to each other on the battlefield."

Lysander was silent while he thought about what his mother had just told him.

"There are only two exceptions to this rule," she continued. "A man can feast and sleep at home on his wedding night - that is when the Gods gifted us with you and Helen - and when he enters a son into the *agoge*. That is tonight and this is why I want everything to be so special for you and for your father… and for you Helen," she added as an afterthought.

In fact, Lysander wasn't sure whether his mother was more excited about the fact that he was about to enter the *agoge* or the fact that his father was visiting their home for his first meal and sleep over in seven years. He thought it was probably his and Helen's coming of age that excited his mother the most but it was a close-run thing. What Lysander didn't know, of course, was that his father did visit the home more often than this but his visits were always late at night and he left before the morning.

Demetria tried once more to get the conversation on a more positive footing. She started to plan out loud in the hope that it would excite Lysander and Helen into joining in.

"For the first course we will have fish," she announced.

"They are not fish though are they?" replied Helen. "They are eels. I don't like eels. They are all slippery and slimy."

Demetria's shoulders sagged a little. Her children were just not in a good mood today. It felt like this was more difficult than it should be. When things went badly she always felt better if she spoke about how wonderful life was in Sparta.

"Shush, Helen," she replied, "you will offend Poseidon. The eels are a gift from the river Eurotas. Poseidon fills the Eurotas with many gifts which he offers to help sustain Sparta. The Eurotas is the finest river in the whole of Greece and you are lucky to eat its bounty."

Helen scowled a little to signal her disagreement. She did not say anything further but she thought to herself, *I wish Poseidon would give us another one of his many gifts, apart from eels all the time.*

"What's for the second course?" asked Lysander.

"Your favourite," said Demetria smiling. Finally, someone had a positive question.

"A mixture of figs, olives, dates, seeds and nuts," she continued. "And as a special treat you will be allowed to drink your first glass of Spartan wine."

She was proud to be a Spartan and she couldn't help adding, "Spartan wine is the finest wine in Greece. Sparta's grapes are the reddest, the plumpest and the juiciest and they make the most excellent wine in all of Greece. In fact, people say that the Gods drink only Spartan wine when they are having a feast."

Lysander licked his lips in anticipation and smiled at the thought that the Gods honoured Sparta in this way. Spartans were extremely religious and always wanted to please the Gods.

"Will I be allowed to drink some?" asked Helen, already knowing what the answer would be.

"Of course not, silly girl," replied Demetria. "You know that Spartan women are not allowed to drink wine until they are sixteen. Why are you asking such silly questions today?"

"It's so unfair," replied Helen. "Sparta needs strong women as well as strong warriors. Wine helps to make you strong, everyone knows that."

"No, it doesn't," her mother responded quickly. "Not at your age. A lot of wine at your age will make you ill. In fact, a lot of wine at any age is not good for you. Lysander will have only one glass tonight as a special treat to mark his passing into the *agoge*. Try not to spoil his special day with your silliness."

This time Lysander tried to change the subject, "...and for the third course?"

His mother smiled with relief. She was pleased to change the subject again.

"It's my favourite," she said. "We will have a pot of roasted birds. There will be pheasant, partridge, quail and ducks. It will be so tasty!"

Demetria licked her lips in anticipation and smiled at Lysander to show that she was thinking of him.

"But that's not all. There's more," she continued. "For our next course we will have your father's favourite - the roasted heart of an ox, cooked in a gravy made out of its own blood. It's a little heavy for my tastes," she continued. "But every Spartan man loves it. It makes you strong in battle and by custom it is at the heart of every *agoge* feast."

Lysander smiled. He'd heard the older men talk fondly of roasted ox heart but he'd never tasted it before. It was a special dish reserved only for special occasions. Indeed, this whole feast was reserved for special occasions. Normally, Spartans ate quite simple meals. But on the evening before the *agoge* they relaxed their normal rules.

"Finally," Demetria concluded. "We will finish with a plate of honey and pine nut cakes. That is, if that clumsy boy Pylos doesn't drop them again!"

Pylos was standing in the corner trying not to be seen while his mother, Lampita, was busying herself with making a fresh batch of honey cakes. When Lysander's mother spoke about his clumsiness again his eyes quickly stared at the floor and his face went red.

V

Demetria shook her head ruefully at the memory of the spilled cakes. It wasn't so much that the cakes had been spoiled - the *helots* could always make more - it was just that she wanted everything to be perfect for Leon's arrival.

She only saw him for the odd snatched moment when he could get away from the common mess. She loved him a lot and she wanted to make tonight perfect for Lysander, Leon and Helen.

Demetria pretended that she was annoyed by Helen's back chat and sharp tongue but, in fact, she was proud of it.

She knew that Spartan women had a reputation throughout the Greek world for being quick witted and biting with their comments. Helen was simply following in that tradition.

In fact, Demetria was proud that Helen was specifically taking after her own mother. A few years ago a famous traveller had conducted a tour around all the Greek city states to compare how they were different from each other. He had been so shocked by how outspoken Spartan women were that he had written down some of the things they said and turned it into a book.

But what made Demetria the proudest of all was that the traveller had even included a quote from her! She had met him at the *agora.* The *agora* was the large public square in the centre of Sparta where public meetings were held. It also sometimes held a market where farmers called *perioikoi* brought their goods so that Spartans could swap extra produce that they didn't need for things that they did need. Sparta did not use money so you couldn't buy and sell things but you could barter and exchange goods. The *perioikoi* received Sparta's protection in return for helping to feed them.

The traveller had spotted Demetria in the *agora* and he had stopped to speak to her. At the time she had been telling off a stallholder for displaying fruit that was past its best. She had not held back in her criticisms. The traveller had listened to this with a smile on his face and when Demetria had stopped he had asked her, "why is it that Spartan women are the only women in Greece to lord it over their men?"

Demetria had looked him firmly in the eye. She did not know who this stranger was. It was clear that he was not Spartan by his clothes and she decided that she didn't like his tone. She answered him quickly. "Because we are the only women in Greece that are mothers of men!"

She meant to imply that all other Greek men were not really men, just boys - including the traveller himself. The traveller understood her meaning straight away.

She had then put her nose in the air and moved on to pick some ripe tomatoes from the next stall. The traveller had laughed nervously but quickly wrote down what she had said. He had then included her reply in his book!

Demetria was very proud of being quoted by the traveller and was very proud that Helen was growing up to be a fine Spartan woman like her mother.... she just wished that Helen would sometimes save her sharp tongue for others.

Demetria stopped her daydreams and clapped her hands again. "Come, your father will be here soon," she announced loudly. "Let's get made up and dressed into our finest clothes."

She paused to make sure she had got everyone's attention. "Lampita, you can help Helen and I get dressed and do our hair. Pylos you can help Lysander put his makeup on... Do you think you can do that without making a mess of it?"

Pylos looked down at his feet again but nodded his head vigorously.

Demetria and Helen went into the anteroom where they usually dressed and Lysander went to his bedroom. As Lysander left he carefully picked up his cloak with the clean and undamaged cakes wrapped up inside.

VI

Lampita started by braiding Helen's hair under Demetria's watchful gaze. This was a complicated and lengthy task. First, she tightly braided Helen's hair from the crown to the nape of her neck and secured it with a small piece of leather, leaving the length free. She then repeated this on the other side of Helen's head and then joined the two lengths together into one long ponytail. Lampita then braided the ponytail and secured it with a piece of silk. The effect was amazing. It totally changed the shape of Helen's face and instantly made her look like a proud Spartan woman of the kind whose faces were pictured on the side of plates and goblets. This was a difficult hairstyle to fashion but Lampita's hands worked quickly and she finished it perfectly. Demetria nodded and smiled. "You can start on my hair now," she said.

VII

Meanwhile, in Lysander's room, the preparations proceeded a lot more quickly. As soon as they entered, Lysander handed the bag of cakes to Pylos. "Quick, hide them in your quarters before my mother finds out," he said. "On your way back, bring me a bowl of warm water and a sponge. That can be your excuse for not being here if my mother sees you."

Pylos smiled briefly at Lysander, nodded and rushed off to hide the cakes and fetch the water. On his return, Lysander quickly washed his own face in the bowl of water. He should really have asked Pylos to do that for him but Lysander wanted to go easy on Pylos. After that he was then ready for Pylos to apply his makeup. This didn't take long. Pylos applied a thick line of black eyeliner under Lysander's eyes. This was the custom for Spartan men and, again, made Lysander look a little older than his seven years of age. Pylos finished the makeup by dabbing Lysander's cheeks with a little pigment made from the mulberry bush to make his cheeks look blushed. Once his makeup was finished, the final touch was to put on his best red tunic and new sandals. Pylos held up the polished brass plate so that Lysander could see his own reflection. Lysander smiled. He looked perfect for his father's arrival. When he became a warrior Lysander would be expected to grow his hair long and put it into ponytails and braid it but the custom for Spartan boys was to have their hair short. So, Lysander was ready quickly and he used the extra time to talk to Pylos about his homeland.

Pylos had never seen Messenia - it had been captured by the Spartans before he was born - but his mother often told him stories about it and Pylos told some of those to Lysander.

It was enjoyable for Lysander to listen to stories about another place. He had never left Sparta and he enjoyed listening to descriptions of far away places. He felt sad for Pylos that his homeland had been captured and that meant he had to be a *helot* for the rest of his life.

VIII

Back in Demetria's room things were progressing more slowly. Once their hair had been braided the next stage was to apply makeup. Strictly speaking, according to the rules set out in the Great Rhetra - or laws of Sparta - it was forbidden for women to wear makeup. However, it was generally accepted that what went on within the privacy of one's own house in Sparta remained a private matter and people often turned a blind eye to such laws in their own house. As a result, women did not wear makeup in public but openly talked about it and applied it in their own home. The makeup applied by Spartan women was similar to that applied by the men. There was a heavy black eyeliner and a red blush applied to the cheeks. First, however, the face had to be painted white. This white powder was made from applying vinegar to lead and then scraping off the powder that slowly formed. Fashions were changing in Sparta, however, and that became a subject of much debate today between Helen and her mother. Older men, like Helen's father, preferred Spartan women to wear makeup when at home. But Helen had overheard a lot of the younger women in the market place talking about how younger Spartan men thought standards in Sparta were slipping and how they wanted to go back to the teachings of the Great Rhetra. As a result, they preferred women to look natural and not wear makeup.

Helen considered herself a thoroughly modern young Spartan woman. She didn't care what other boys thought of her but she did want to fit in with the other young women and so she really did not want to wear makeup. She liked the idea of being a proper Spartan.

Demetria became very upset when Helen explained all this to her.

"But your father will want to see you in makeup looking your best for his arrival. Please, Helen, just agree to let Lampita put a little makeup on your face."

"No, she's not coming near me with that stuff - it smells bad too," said Helen.

There was a long pause. Demetria looked defeated and she could tell that Helen intended to stand her ground. Demetria began to cry a little at the thought that Helen was going to spoil Lysander's big day and Leon's arrival at home.

"Look what you've made me do, Helen," she said. "Lampita will have to wash my face and start all over again."

Demetria paused. She thought for a moment and then an idea came to her. She turned to Helen with a hopeful look on her face.

"Helen," she said. "I have a suggestion."

She waited a moment or two and then continued. "Tonight is a special night and I don't want you to spoil it. I know that you don't like eels. So, here is my offer……this will be the last time that I ask you to wear makeup - ever - and, if you agree, I will ask Lampita to give you a portion of eels without any eels in it - just the vegetables. Your father will never know. How does that sound?"

Helen thought carefully about the offer. She could see that her mother was upset and she didn't want to upset her further or to spoil things.

"I agree," she said. "But not that horrible white powder that smells of vinegar."

"Agreed," said her mother.

After the makeup was finished the rest of the preparations went more smoothly. Spartan women wore a dress called a *chiton*. It fastened on one side over the shoulder and left the other shoulder bare. It was just a question of choosing their finest *chitons* and their best sandals.

Demetria chose a white *chiton* edged with purple and Helen chose another white *chiton* but edged with thin gold braid. Helen also sported a thin, twisted leather belt around her waist. The belt was not to hold her *chiton* up but because a twisted leather belt was the latest fashion that she had seen in the marketplace.

IX

Finally, the time arrived. Lysander's and Helen's father, Leon, came home. They saw him coming along the path through their vegetable garden before he spotted them. Their vegetable garden was big but the same size as everyone else's. Sparta had been designed in this way. The land had been divided into nine thousand equal shares. It meant that everyone had the same amount of land so that no-one could be jealous of anybody else. Demetria had turned their plot of land into a large vegetable garden and this meant that they had a plentiful supply of fresh vegetables.

Leon looked happy and fit. What was more he was clearly carrying some gifts - and some quite large gifts at that. Everything was wrapped in cloth so they couldn't see what was inside but there were at least two large bundles and one of them was very long.

Leon spotted them as he approached the house. He stopped, put down the bundles and waved at them.

"Go inside, children," he shouted. "I want these presents to be a surprise. Go join your mother and I will put these safe until later. I'll be inside in a moment."

Lysander and Helen did as they were asked and excitedly told Demetria that Father was home.

X

Leon was as good as his word. It was only a short moment before he came bounding in the door and opened his arms to greet them all. He had a flask of wine in one hand but there was no time to hand it over before everyone rushed him and hugged him as tightly as they could.

Once the excitement subsided a little he handed the flask of wine to Demetria with a hug and a kiss just for her. "It's a special wine for tonight. A flask of *Lacedaemia's* finest," he said. "For the feast."

This use of the word "*Lacedaemia*" sounded odd to Lysander's ears. He didn't hear it said often but he knew that *Lacedaemia* was the name for the wider region conquered and occupied by the Spartans. Sparta was the name of their capital city and that was the name they were known by to most other Greeks. If someone referred to Sparta as *Lacedaemia* they were showing that they were proud of Sparta's conquests and its wider territory. His father, Leon, was clearly one of those people.

"You all look fantastic," he said. "Helen, your makeup looks beautiful. You are going to make a fine *Lacedaemian* woman. And you, Lysander.

Look at you. You are going to make a fine warrior. You are going to help defend and expand *Lacedaemia* and you are going to make your mother and I proud."

Helen, Lysander and Demetria all beamed at these compliments and Helen was glad that, in the end, she had agreed to her mother's request.

Before the feast began properly they all sat and chatted.

"Come tell me all the news," said Leon.

The family sat and talked excitedly.

They told him all about the latest comings and goings: what was happening with their neighbours; what gossip they had heard in the market; what repairs needed doing on the house; and how there was so much work to do that Demetria was thinking of getting another *helot*. After all, Lampita was getting old and tending to the vegetable garden was getting too much for her.

Leon nodded. "We'll look into that," he said.

In return, Leon told them all about the latest news from across Greece and the latest political intrigue. He had picked all this up from the talk in the common mess and the weekly assembly.

"I've heard that Thebes is expanding its army," he said. "I've also heard that Corinth is getting rich from all the trade in grain coming into its port from Asia Minor. People are saying that Corinthian soldiers are getting fat and lazy and, as a result, there is talk in the assembly of launching an attack on Corinth. I think this is just gossip though and hot heads talking because, of course, the biggest threat remains, as always, Athens."

"Why is Athens our biggest threat, Father?" asked Lysander.

Lysander realised that now he was to become a man he needed to understand such things and to join in such conversations.

"Athens is the largest of the Greek city states," Leon replied. "They are jealous of *Lacedaemia* and would like to conquer us. We always need to be on our guard against them. *Lacedaemion* spies have reported that Athens is building up its navy again. Athens knows it cannot defeat *Lacedaemia* in a fair fight on land so it always tries to dominate the seas. If they are building a bigger navy, that can mean only one thing. Athens must be preparing to attack again. It's just a question of who they are planning to attack."

Lysander nodded.

"So, even though there is talk of attacking Corinth," Leon continued. "I think it would be unwise for *Lacedaemia* to go to war with anyone until we are clear where Athens' intentions lie."

Lysander listened to all this talk with the utmost interest. He busily soaked up all his father told him.

Helen also started off by paying attention. She knew that, as a Spartan woman, she would have the right to attend and speak at the assembly. So, she wanted to ask what legal matters had been brought before the assembly because she thought that would make her look clever in front of her father. But her father talked so quickly that she didn't get the chance and slowly her interest waned.

Eventually, she plucked up the courage and interrupted, "All this talk of war is scaring me, Father. Can we talk about something else please?"

Leon looked at her - a little surprised. He paused and thought for a while.

"So, talk of war and politics is boring to you, is it? Perhaps, we should talk about philosophy or poetry instead? What do you think of that?"

Helen looked blankly at her father as she didn't really know what philosophy was and she found poetry a bit boring. She wondered if they might be more interesting to talk about than war but they didn't sound promising.

"There's talk of a new philosopher arriving in Athens," he continued. "I think his name is Anaxagoras or something like that. His home town has just been captured by the Persians and so he has come to Athens to escape them. Would that be more interesting to you instead?"

Helen rolled her eyes and let out a little click with her tongue. Leon was tricking Helen, of course. He knew she would not understand about philosophy and the news about

Anaxagoras was just a way to keep talking about politics. Leon believed that *Lacedaemions* had no use for such things as philosophy. Fighting, military training and politics were the only subjects that should interest a good *Lacedaemion*. But he didn't want to tell his daughter off or upset her as he hadn't seen her in such a long time.

Helen rolled her eyes again. "Okay, let's keep talking about war then," she said. "At least I know what that is all about."

Leon smiled in response. He composed himself and put on his serious face again.

"Talking of the Persians," he said. "That is the most worrying development of all. The latest news is that they have a new Emperor. He is called Xerxes.... I have a bad feeling about Xerxes."

"Why?" asked Lysander.

"Well," his father replied. "Xerxes is the son of Darius and Darius was no friend of *Lacedaemia*. It remains to be seen what he will do but I would not be surprised to find that he will return to *Lacedaemia* to try to recover some of his father's honour after we defeated him last time. The Persians will not forget our last victory over them and I think they will be back to avenge themselves. They have already started to reconquer parts of Asia Minor - that's why Anaxagoras had to flee. So, they are already flexing their muscles and starting to expand again."

He paused for dramatic effect. "That's why it's so important," he continued. "That Lysander enters the *agoge* tomorrow and joins the *Lacedaemion* army."

And with that, Demetria clapped her hands and exclaimed, "all this talk of war is making me hungry. It's time to eat. Let's move to the table and get Lampita and Pylos to bring out the first course."

XI

So, Lampita and Pylos brought out the first course of food. As Demetria had promised, it was fish - or more precisely, as Helen had observed, it was eels. Also, as Demetria had promised, Helen's portion contained only vegetables. Helen smiled to herself and congratulated herself on her negotiating skills. No eels and no more makeup. This was turning into a good day for her.

"Eat up, both of you," said Leon. "Tomorrow is a really important day for both of you. You will stop being children and you will start to contribute to the future health and prosperity of *Lacedaemia*."

Both Lysander and Helen looked intently at their father. They were unsure of what would come next. Demetria had spoken to them both about this in some detail but they wanted to hear what their father had to say on the subject.

He seemed to be even more knowledgeable about this than their mother.

"Lysander, you will begin the process of training to be a *Lacedaemian* hoplite - the greatest warriors in the whole of Greece. You will start in the *agoge* and I will talk to you later this evening about what this will entail. I will tell you what to expect and will give you some advice."

Lysander nodded.

"Helen," Leon continued. "You will train to become a *Lacedaemian* woman. You will learn to be the fittest, quickest, most intelligent and most healthy of all the women in Greece. You will marry a fine *Lacedaemian* man and you will create a family that will produce the next citizens of *Lacedaemia*. This is a great responsibility that you bear."

Helen wasn't sure about this. Spartan boys didn't interest her. They seemed weak and silly and she had no desire to make babies with them. But she decided not to contradict her father for the moment.

"Your training will begin early in the morning. Your trainer will be a woman called Gorga. Your mother has chosen Gorga because she trained your mother and your mother, of course, is the finest woman in the whole of *Lacedaemia*." He said this last bit with a playful smile on his lips. "So, you can be confident that Gorga will do a great job. Do you have any questions?"

Lysander and Helen shook their heads. They both had lots of questions but now didn't seem the right moment to ask them.

"Good," said Demetria, still smiling from the compliment that her husband had paid her. "Let's have the next course."

XII

Lampita and Pylos brought out the next course. This was a mixture of figs, olives, dates, seeds and nuts. It was not a lot of food but it had lots of different flavours and was designed to increase the appetite for the meat dishes to follow.

Helen had been thinking about the news that she was to be trained by Gorga and a question now formed on her lips. "What will my training consist of please, Mother?"

Demetria smiled.

"That is a good question, Helen," she replied. "Let me see, when I was a girl your age, the training was based around five key disciplines."

Demetria remembered hard and listed out each of the five priorities on her fingers.

"They are: athletic prowess, hunting, dancing, singing and studies such as mathematics, geometry and writing - Lysander you will also learn mathematics and writing."

Helen thought about this for a moment. "Dancing and singing. Do I really have to learn those things? They sound silly to me."

Demetria smiled another broad smile. "I thought you might say that. You may think dancing and singing are not very important but I predict that you will end up enjoying those two things the most."

"I doubt it," replied Helen.

"Why do you say that?" asked her mother.

Helen declined to answer. She didn't want to upset her mother, so she chose to say nothing. Demetria, however, was having none of it.

"Well, let me tell you about dancing first," she continued. "The dance is important because it is used to celebrate Spartan victories. So, you will need to learn it in order to show our returning warriors that their sacrifice and their effort is appreciated. But more importantly, it is really a form of gymnastics. The best dance is called the *bibasis*. To do it well you need to jump high in the air and kick your own buttocks from behind. The higher you can jump and the louder the slap you can make against your buttocks the better it is. You land once and then immediately jump and kick again. It makes your legs extremely strong and it will make you super fit. There is also a competition each year for the *bibasis* dancer who can jump the most times in a row. The record last year was exactly one thousand jumps. The girl got to one thousand and then collapsed. But the winner of the annual *bibasis* competition has her image painted onto a plate. You are always saying that you want the chance to be famous like Lysander. Well, the *bibasis* is your chance."

Helen smiled a big smile and jumped high into the air and kicked her buttocks from behind.

"Very good," said her mother. "You might be a natural."

Helen tried again to do a series of jumps. But as soon as she landed and tried to jump again she pitched forward and nearly smashed into the table. She tried again, with the same effect.

"Maybe you should wait until Gorga has taught you how to do it properly," suggested her mother.

"Let me tell you about the singing next. You're going to like this even more. There are two types of singing. First, there are the songs that must be sung before our warriors go off to battle. These songs must be beautiful to remind the men of what they will miss about Sparta and why they must be victorious so that they will fight hard to come back. These songs are very important... But the second type of songs are the ones you will like the most. They are called *ridicule songs*."

Helen felt she needed to interrupt.

"Ridicule songs?" she asked with a quizzical tone.

"Yes," replied her mother. "You will get to watch the boys training in the *agoge* and you may even compete against them. Any that you think are not trying hard enough you must make a note of their names. Then in front of all the public dignitaries at the monthly festival you will be invited to sing a song about those boys to say how bad or lazy they have been and how they need to try harder. You are expected to shame them and the more hurtful and cruel your song, the better it will be."

Helen could not believe her ears. "Yes," she cried with joy, "I can't wait to sing about Lysander!"

Lysander instantly looked hurt. "You will never get to sing a song about me, Helen. I will make sure of that," he said with steady determination in his voice.

"Yes," said Demetria. "You can sing about Lysander if he fails but he will not fail. He will not let this family or Sparta down. I am sure of that."

"Let's eat our food now," said Leon. "I am starving."

So the family settled down to the second course. Helen could not have been happier and Lysander was now a little worried about his sister and her cruel songs.

XIII

The next course was all the wild fowl. Lysander thought they were each a little small but once he had eaten three or four he started to fill up.

"Good," said Leon. "Eat up. You need to build your strength for the *agoge*. It will not be easy."

Lysander had been waiting patiently for his father to tell him all about the *agoge*, especially as listening about Helen's training had now made him nervous. He decided he couldn't wait any longer.

"What will happen in the *agoge*?" he asked impatiently.

Leon looked long and hard at him. After a little while, he gave him the following answer, "Each boy's experience of the *agoge* is different as it depends on the boy and the other boys who join. Those boys will be your companions for the next twenty-three years. The men I eat with in the common mess all joined the *agoge* as boys with me at the same time. We are now like brothers to each other."

Lysander nodded.

"There are only three rules I will give you," Leon continued. "To help you make the best of your time in the *agoge.* The first is: make friends with the other members of your pack. You will meet them tomorrow and you must form a strong bond with them as soon as possible. The second is: always put the needs of the group above the needs of yourself. If you put your own needs first you will be seen as selfish and weak. The third, and most important, is: never feel self-pity. The moment you feel sorry for yourself is the moment you will have let yourself down and failed *Lacedaemia*. Think of the little bird who dies of hunger and cold in the dead of winter. How much self-pity do you think the little bird feels in the moments before it dies?"

Lysander had not thought about this question and so had no answer for his father.

"None. Not one ounce of self-pity," Leon quickly explained. "The little bird will put all of its energy into surviving. It will continue to fight for its life until its very last breath. You must do the same."

Lysander nodded but he couldn't help feeling a little scared at this advice.

"Come," said Demetria. "This is serious stuff. The boy will learn soon enough. Let's keep our mood and the feast a little lighter tonight."

Leon nodded.

"Bring on the ox's heart then!" He gave a huge laugh, which broke the tension in the room so that everyone laughed in agreement.

XIV

Lampita brought out the roasted ox heart to great applause and placed it in the centre of the table. Leon declared with pride, "I will carve."

He proceeded to carve fine slices for everyone but it was clear that the slices he cut for Lysander were bigger and thicker than everyone else's. When Leon had finished carving he announced, "I think it's time for Lysander to taste his first drink of *Lacedaemon* wine. Lampita bring us the flask that I brought earlier, and three glasses. Also, bring some water for Helen."

Only the slightest furrowing of Helen's brow was visible but she knew better than to make a fuss now. She was determined to taste the wine though and started to think about how she could get some.

Lysander first tasted the roasted ox heart. The meat was chewy and the flavour heavy and rich. He wasn't sure he liked it but he made sure he ate the whole plateful. He then raised the glass of wine to his lips and took his first sip. It tasted oily and bitter in his mouth. It burned the back of his throat and stung his mouth. He did not like the taste at all but he made sure that he swallowed it all down. The taste it left in his mouth was not good and he decided that wine was not something he was going to drink again for a long time.

"How does it taste Lysander?" his mother asked.

"It's nice," he lied. "But a little bitter."

"Don't worry," said his mother. "The honey and pine nut cakes are sweet and will take away that taste. Would you like them now?"

Lysander nodded.

"Yes, please."

And so Lampita brought in the second tray of cakes that she had baked. Pylos asked to be excused from this duty as he did not want to drop the plate again. His mother agreed.

And so the family meal ended. Lysander was absolutely full and felt very happy to have his whole family sitting around the table and talking so well together.

XV

"Time for some presents," Leon declared. "Just wait there and I will fetch them."

Leon disappeared and came back with two large bundles. While he was gone the *helots* started to clear away the meal and Helen offered to help. Normally this would be work that the *helots* would do themselves so Helen quickly explained to everyone, "I am stiff. I need to stretch."

She collected all the dirty crockery including Lysander's wine glass and the flask of wine, which still had two little drops of wine left in the bottom. As she got into the kitchen she poured the dregs into the glass and drank the remaining wine in a single gulp. She waited a second to see how it would taste and feel.

After a brief pause, she pulled her head back and let out a small noise. She couldn't believe how awful it tasted! It burned her mouth and then her tummy and made her screw up her face.

She had only just regained her composure and returned to the dining room when her father returned with the presents.

Leon unwrapped the first cloth bundle. Inside it was a large bronze shield and a bronze helmet. The shield was painted white on the front except for a thin strip all the way around the outside that remained bronze. In the middle of the white circle there was a big upside down letter V. The letter was the shape of an upside down V but it did not represent the letter V. It represented the letter *Lamda* or L in Greek. And, of course, Lamda or L stood for *Lacedaemia*.

Leon handed them both to Lysander. The shield was as tall as he was when it rested on the ground and the helmet was so big that it immediately went down below his shoulders and completely covered his head so that he couldn't see. The shield was so heavy he couldn't pick it up and, indeed, as soon as his father let go of it, it started to topple towards the floor as he couldn't hold it up.

"I know these are too big for you now but let me explain," said his father gently chuckling to himself. "A father always hands on his armour to his son once he has finished being a warrior. But I am still part of the hoplite phalanx and I will continue to serve *Lacedaemia* until I am sixty years old. Therefore, you cannot have my armour until I have retired. Every father therefore has two sets of armour so that he can pass on a set to his son when he graduates from the *agoge.* You will also get my current set when I retire so that you can hand it to your son. My second set is as good as my own armour. It last saw action in the wars against the Messenians when they tried to revolt and is still in very good condition."

Lysander tried not to show it on his face but he flashed a glance at Pylos. He remembered that Pylos had told him his mother's home was Messenia so his family had become *helots* as a result of the Messenian campaign. Lysander felt a little ashamed to be given these presents in front of Pylos but excited that he was inheriting such armour from his father.

Lysander's father continued, "You will not take these to the *agoge* with you. They will stay here at home until you have reached eighteen and you join the army properly. They will be handed to you at your passing out ceremony. However, I wanted you to see and feel them so that you know what you are training for."

"Thank you," said Lysander. "They are beautiful."

"Wait, there's more," said his father.

He left again and came back with a long thin present wrapped in cloth. He unfolded the cloth slowly to reveal a beautifully made spear.

"Again, this is too big for you now," his father explained. "But this will be your main weapon in the phalanx. It is called a *xyston*. You will kill many Persians with this *xyston* when the time comes - or Athenians if they try to defeat us again. Here, feel the weight and the balance of it.

You will fall in love with your *xyston* and it will save your life many times."

Lysander picked up the spear. It was enormous and he could hardly lift it. It was eight feet long and so was a good two feet taller than his father. The handle was smoothly polished though and he could feel that it was perfectly balanced in the middle.

"It's fantastic, Father," he said excitedly.

Throughout all of this Helen had been sitting quietly watching. Now she felt she had to speak up. For reasons she couldn't explain she was feeling a bit more confident than usual and so she decided to speak her mind.

"I know it's Lysander's special day but it's my special day, too. Do I get any presents?"

She knew the answer would be no but she wanted to ask just to make the point that girls always got forgotten when anything exciting happened.

Her father gave a wry smile. "What do you think?" he asked.

Helen fell silent. She wanted to say - "*I'll bet you didn't get me anything as Lysander is your favourite because he's a boy.*"

But she realised that would not sound good so she just stayed silent.

"Well, as a matter of fact," said her father. "I did get you something. Wait here."

XVI

Leon disappeared and came back shortly with another parcel wrapped in cloth. It was not as big as the ones he had brought for Lysander but it was still a reasonable size.

"First, I have a question," said her father. "Who makes the finest bows in all of Greece?"

"That's easy," replied Helen. "Everyone knows that Cretan archers are the best because they train the most and have the best bows."

"Very good," replied Leon, and with that he handed her the present.

Helen slowly unwrapped it and to her astonishment she discovered that it contained a small hunting bow and six perfectly made arrows.

"I wasn't sure what to get you," Leon said. "At first I thought about getting you a lyre because you will learn to make music and sing, as your mother explained. But, somehow, I just felt that that wouldn't excite you enough. Although now, having listened to your mother, I wonder whether I was wrong about that. Anyway, I remembered that you will also learn how to hunt. I remembered that we found a child's hunting bow among the treasures taken during the Messenian campaigns and someone said this bow was Cretan. So, it should be good enough for you to use now. Do you like it?"

Helen nodded enthusiastically and rushed up to hug her father with the biggest hug he had had all night.

"Your father is so kind," said Demetria. "But I fear that we should draw a close to our feast tonight. Lysander, you must rise at the fifth hour tomorrow to join the *agoge* and Helen, your tutor Gorga will be here at the seventh hour."

"I will rise with you Lysander," said his father. "And take you to the *agoge*. Let's all get some sleep now."

CHAPTER II
First day in the agoge

I

Leon gently shook Lysander to wake him up.

"Come, it is time to go to the *agoge*," he said. "Get dressed and I will meet you at the front door."

Lysander rubbed the sleep from his eyes. He looked out of the window and saw that the sun had yet to rise. He knew from experience that it must be early, even before the fifth hour in the morning.

Although Sparta was a hot country, especially in the summer, it could get quite cool during the night as well as in the winter. He felt the chill in the air and shivered a little. Rising from his bed he put on his tunic and his sandals and grabbed his cloak that was hanging on the back of the door. Wrapping the cloak tightly around himself he felt the warm protection that it offered.

His father rubbed Lysander's hair with affection when he met him outside the door.

"Come," he said. "You have a big day ahead of you. Do you remember my advice?"

"Yes," replied Lysander. "Make friends with the other boys, never put myself first and never feel self-pity."

His father smiled.

"Very good. Well done. You are going to make a fine warrior."

And with that his father started to walk towards the outskirts of Sparta.

In the beginning Sparta had just been a collection of villages. As it had grown bigger some spaces of open ground had still been left between the old villages. These open spaces had often been taken over by nature and were filled with wild olive trees or other kinds of grasses or bushes. Beyond these old villages were the fields of the *perioikoi*.

Lysander followed a few steps behind his father. After a while they came to an area of relatively flat scrub near the edge of town. It was covered in grass that was brown from the summer heat. A few olive trees were scattered here and there. The sun was only just coming up but Lysander could tell these trees would offer some patches of shade when the sun reached its highest and hottest point.

Lysander wondered why his father had stopped.

"We are here," his father announced.

Lysander looked around in confusion.

"Here? Aren't we going to an academy?"

It was well-known that an academy was the place where festivals were held and where much training took place. Lysander had expected to be taken either directly to an academy or somewhere close to one.

"No," replied his father. "You are still young. You are joining the *paides*. I was told to bring you here to Mentos Field and the other *paides* should start to arrive soon."

His father had used the formal name for his group, the *paides*. Just like he referred to Sparta as *Lacedaemia*. Most people referred to the *paides* as the *cub pack*. It was the group of boys that entered the *agoge* at the age of seven and they would stay in the *paides* until the age of twelve.

II

At that very moment, Lysander saw another boy being brought into the patch of grassland by a man, who he assumed must be the boy's father. The pair walked over to them and the man turned to the boy.

"Introduce yourself," he said gently.

"I am Polydoros," said the boy. "I am joining the *agoge* today."

"I am Lysander. I am also joining the *agoge*," Lysander replied.

Lysander looked at Polydoros.

He was a little taller than Lysander and he looked a little stronger. Lysander also noticed that Polydoros did not look at him. Polydoros just had a faint smile on his face - more of a leer - and looked down at the ground all the time. There was something about Polydoros that Lysander didn't like but he couldn't put his finger exactly on what it was.

There was no time for further conversation or speculation though as two more boys soon arrived. One was alone while the other was accompanied by an adult.

"I am Teleklos," said the first boy who was accompanied.

Teleklos was of medium build and had a mop of dark hair on his head. He was not close shaven as most Spartan boys his age were.

"And I am Leobotas," said the lone boy.

Leobotas was a big strong boy, even bigger than Polydoros and he did not look at the ground. In fact, his gaze did not flinch as he looked each boy over in turn to see what their strengths and weaknesses might be. He looked straight at Lysander and gave a wry smile as he stared him in the eye. Again, Lysander felt uncomfortable at the way that Leobotas looked at him.

The other four boys arrived shortly after that. Three were accompanied by adults and another was not.

The first boy introduced himself as Leon.

Lysander shot a glance at his father and said proudly, "Leon. That's my father's name."

His father gave a brief smile but did not speak. This was the time for the boys to introduce themselves, not for the fathers to socialise.

Leon the cub was small and clearly a little shy. His face went bright red as soon as Lysander spoke to him. Nonetheless, he gave Lysander a smile in return for his favourable comment about him sharing his name with Lysander's father. He reached his hand forward and shook hands with Lysander.

"Good to meet you, son of Leon," the young Leon said. He then quickly stood back and looked at the ground with his face glowing red.

The next boy was called Pausarius. His face was dirty and his hair was unkempt but worst of all his nose was running down his face in two large, thick streams. Pausarius didn't seem to be bothered by his running nose and let it continue. Lysander's stomach turned slightly and he found it hard to even look at Pausarius.

The next boy, who was also unaccompanied, was called Ariston.

"Hello," said Lysander.

He recognised Ariston as someone he had played with in the past. He thought that his mother and Ariston's mother might even be friends as he had been to Ariston's house when they were younger. Ariston clearly recognised Lysander and smiled, returning his greeting warmly.

Lysander wondered why two of the boys had come alone but he did not feel that now was the right time to ask.

The last boy was called Charillos, who was a

little chubby and tripped as he entered the grassy area. He laughed so as to make a joke of it but none of the other boys were amused. They were all very serious.

Lysander could feel Leobotas's eyes still boring into him and he felt a little uneasy.

The boys stood around in a circle getting the measure of each other but not saying very much. Their fathers stood back outside the circle and just watched on as the boys waited for what would come next.

III

They didn't have long to wait. A short while passed since Charillos had arrived. At this point, a young teenage Spartan arrived at the grassy field dressed in full armour with two *helots* pulling a small cart behind him.

The young warrior strode into the middle of the field and spoke in a loud voice, "Greetings *paides* or new cubs. Welcome to your first day in the *agoge*. Fathers who have brought their sons to the *agoge* - Sparta thanks you. You are making the ultimate sacrifice for the future of Sparta by giving up your boys to training. You will be rewarded with a long and happy life in a Sparta kept safe by these boys. You may now leave them."

At that, all the fathers turned on their heels and left as one. They did not wave to their sons or say anything. They just marched away.

IV

The young Spartan warrior spoke again. "Greetings again *paides*. I am Nikandros. I am your *paidiskoi*. I am in the second phase of my training and I will be your mentor and guide through the *agoge*. Those of you who survive will become *paidiskoi* when you reach the age of twelve. Until then you have five years and much to learn. You will follow my instructions and that of any other *paidiskoi* that I bring to speak to you. Do you understand?"

The boys all nodded in unison.

"You will not take orders from anyone else. Unless you make a mistake. In which case, I will send you to the *ephors*, who will be responsible for your punishment. Do you understand?"

Once again, the boys all nodded in unison.

"Let me hear you," shouted Nikandros.

The boys were a little uneasy and some shifted on their feet but they all replied with varying degrees of loudness.

"Yes, we understand, Nikandros."

"Good," said Nikandros. "I want you all to take off your civilian clothes. You must put that life behind you now. Strip naked and put the clothes from your old life in a pile here."

He pointed to a spot under one of the olive trees. The boys were a little unsure at first of what to do and Lysander wondered if he had heard Nikandros properly. He started to realise that Nikandros was serious and that this was a ritual way of separating his future in the *agoge* from his past life at home.

But Leobotas and Polydoros had worked this out before him and they had already started to remove their clothes and put them in the spot that Nikandros had indicated. Either they had worked it out or they were just very good at following orders, thought Lysander.

Nonetheless, the other boys, including Lysander, started to follow suit. Soon they were all standing naked apart from a small loin cloth around their private parts.

There were two exceptions to this. The first was Pausarius who wasn't wearing a loin cloth under his tunic and so was already completely naked. He still had his two nose streams but he was standing firmly to attention with a very serious look on his face.

The second was Charillos; who was hesitating. It seemed that he didn't want to remove his tunic in front of the other boys. He was a little self-conscious about the extra weight that he was carrying.

Nikandros approached Charillos and put his face very close to his. In a soft, low voice he asked, "What is your name, cub?"

"Ch-Charillos," Charillos replied.

"Well, Ch-Charillos, do you want me to send

you to the *ephors* on your very first day? I met the chief *ephor* this morning and he was in a very bad mood. He said he hadn't had a chance to use his beating stick for over a week and he was getting impatient. Shall we go to see him together?"

Charillos let out a little whimper but at that he did as he was asked. He whipped off his tunic and stood with the other boys standing only in their loin clothes - or in Pausarius's case - completely naked.

"Good," declared Nikandos. "I will now leave you for one hour. When I return I will give you your equipment. During the time that I am gone I want you to elect a leader who will speak on your behalf. I will speak to you through your leader. Do you understand? Do not let it be Charillos. He will bring shame on you until we have toughened him up. Do you understand?"

"Yes, Nikandros," the boys replied.

With that Nikandros turned on his heels and marched away from the field, with the *helots* still pulling the cart behind them.

V

The boys all stood around for a few moments not knowing how to begin. Finally, it was Leobotas who spoke up, "I think I should be the leader," he said. "I am the strongest and my father was killed fighting the Athenians so my family knows what it is to make a sacrifice for Sparta."

There was a small pause while all the boys thought about what Leobotas had said. It was Ariston who replied first. "But my father died fighting the Persians. The Persians are Sparta's biggest enemy and so if you are using that reason then I should be given a chance to be leader. Perhaps we should put it to a vote between the two of us?"

Leobotas snarled with an ugly look on his face. He paused for a moment and then, without saying a word, he took a step forward and smashed Leon in the face. It was not Ariston, who had spoken against him, that he struck. Instead, Leobotas struck Leon - a boy who had said nothing. The blow took Leon completely by surprise as he had given no indication that he was any kind of threat to Leobotas. It caught him square on his nose and instantly floored him.

Leon dropped to his knees holding his nose as blood poured from it. Leon knew that a true Spartan did not show pain but he could not help it. He screamed and then cried small sobs of pain as he clutched his face tightly with both hands.

The other boys looked on with their mouths gaping open in surprise. They couldn't quite believe what they had just seen.

"We are not taking a vote," Leobotas said firmly. "We are not Athenians and we don't believe in democracy. I said that I should be the leader because I am the strongest. I have just shown you that I am prepared to take action. So, if you want to challenge me to be the leader, you will have to fight me."

It didn't take Ariston long to think about this. He quickly put up his hands to fight Leobotas like he had seen the boxers do. But Leobotas was too quick and he didn't fight fair. He stepped forward again and grabbed Ariston around the neck. He kicked Ariston's legs from under him so that he fell to his knees and he began to apply a strong headlock around Ariston's throat.

All this happened so quickly that Lysander didn't know how to react. Lysander knew that he liked Ariston and that if he didn't do something Leobotas was going to make him pass out, or worse, kill him. He also didn't think Leobotas would make a good leader as he seemed to think a lot of himself and so was breaking his father's second rule.

Lysander at this point was slightly behind Leobotas and Ariston, who was struggling wildly to break free from Leobotas's grip. Lysander stepped forward and landed the hardest punch he could manage on the back of Leobotas's head.

Lysander's punch had three effects. Firstly, it stopped Leobotas strangling Ariston. Leobotas loosened his grip and put his hands to the back of his own head in pain. Secondly, Lysander hadn't really appreciated how hard the back of the skull was. He hadn't formed a proper fist and so when he smashed the back of Leobotas's head he had really hurt his own fist. He heard a loud crack as the bones in his hand reacted to being hit into what felt like a brick wall. Lysander winced with the pain and stumbled backwards cradling his damaged hand with his other hand. Thirdly, Lysander's actions helped to make up Polydoros's and Teleklos's minds. They decided it would be safer if they sided with Leobotas and give him their support. As a result, they sprung forward and pinned Lysander to the ground. He didn't resist much but they still punched him a little to make sure that he didn't fight back.

VI

It was all over in a few moments. Ariston was red in the face and holding his throat where Leobotas had strangled him. Leon was still trying to stop the blood that was flowing from his nose. Lysander was pinned to the ground with Polydoros and Teleklos on top of him. That left only Pausarius and Charillos, who had yet to do anything. Leobotas turned to them both and shouted in a menacing voice. "Anybody else want to challenge me?"

They both quickly shook their heads and raised their hands in submission.

"Good," said Leobotas. "That's settled then. When Nikandros returns I will explain that I am the leader."

With that over the boys settled down to wait

for Nikandros. They separated into two groups a little distance apart. The first group contained Leobotas, Polydoros, Teleklos, Pausarius and Charillos and they quietly chatted about what might happen next when Nikandros came back.

The second smaller group contained Lysander, Ariston and Leon. They were much quieter as they tended to their wounds.

Ariston whispered to Lysander, "Thank you."

But Lysander barely heard it through a mixture of the pain in his own hand and his concern for Leon who was still bleeding.

Lysander went across to the pile of clothes that were still heaped up under the olive tree. He found his own tunic and ripped a little strip off. Tearing this strip into two he returned to where Leon was gently sobbing.

"Here," he murmured. "Use these to stop the blood coming from your nose. We will clean the wound when the bleeding has stopped."

Leon nodded weakly and pushed the two strips of cloth into his nostrils.

VII

Demetria gently rocked Helen awake by pushing her shoulder. "Come," she said. "It is time for you to get up. Gorga will be here shortly."

Helen nodded and slowly started to rise from her bed to get dressed for the day ahead.

"I have arranged for you to spend the day

with Gorga in a quiet corner of the courtyard," said her mother. "You will be undisturbed there. I will go to the market this morning so that you have the house to yourself and you can get to know Gorga a little more. I think you will like her. There's some yoghurt, fruits and nuts left over from the feast last night. You can eat those for breakfast."

Helen did as her mother suggested. She asked Pylos to bring her some breakfast, said goodbye to her mother as she left for the market and then waited patiently for Gorga to arrive.

It took about half an hour before there was a loud knock on the door. Lampita scuttled forth and opened it to find an oldish woman about her own age standing outside.

"I am Gorga," the woman announced. "I am here to train Helen."

"Yes, of course, Mistress Gorga," said Lampita. "Follow me into the courtyard and I will fetch Helen for you."

Gorga followed Lampita to the courtyard, made herself comfortable and awaited Helen's arrival.

Lampita fetched Helen. She stood facing Gorga but did not say anything. Gorga was a little older and a little smaller than Helen had expected.

"Are you Helen?" Gorga asked.

"Yes," replied Helen. "You must be Gorga."

"I am," she replied. "And you are skinnier

than I had expected. You also look like you are a silly, badly behaved girl."

Helen stared at her, surprised by her harsh tone. Especially as they had only just met. Helen wasn't sure what to say in reply.

"Why do you think I am here?" Gorga asked.

"You are here to train me," Helen replied. "You trained my mother and you have agreed to train me as a favour to my mother because you are loyal to her and you love her."

"Wrong," replied Gorga. "Your mother was as silly and useless as you are. I have no loyalty or love for her. I am here because Sparta requires me to be here. My role is to train you so that you grow up to be fit and strong and less silly than you are now. I do not want to be here. I am required to be here. And let's be clear, I do not like you and I am not your friend."

This is going to be a tough day, thought Helen.

VIII

It was not too long before Nikandros returned with the *helots*. He took the scene in with a single glance - the two groups and the injured boys in one.

"Have you chosen a leader?" he asked.

Leobotas stood up.

"Yes, it is going to be me," he said. "My name is Leobotas."

"Good," replied Nikandros. "Is that a

unanimous decision? Do you have the support of all your pack?"

The boys all remained silent. The group that was sitting with Leobotas nodded their agreement. But it was clear that some of the group - those sitting away from Leobotas - did not support him for leader. However, none of those who disagreed wanted to draw attention to themselves, so they remained silent.

"I need to hear what you boys think," said Nikandros. "Do you support Leobotas as your leader?"

It took a few moments of uncomfortable silence during which Nikandros waited patiently for an answer. The boys remained silent.

"Well?" he asked, after a little while.

Slowly, Ariston and then Lysander, followed by Leon, shook their heads. It was clear that they didn't want Leobotas as their leader.

"Very well," said Nikandros. "You have learnt your first lesson cubs. Leadership is important in the Spartan army. The leader must be able to command the loyalty of his men so that they do what he asks of them in the heat of battle. But a leader must command the loyalty of all his men, not just some of them. Otherwise, he is a bad leader and there is no room for bad leaders in the Spartan army."

Leobotas looked visibly confused and deflated. He thought he had done well by putting himself forward as leader and that he would get special privileges as a result. But instead here he was being told that he was a bad leader. All because that stupid Ariston and Lysander had not accepted his leadership. He understood that Leon did not support him yet because he had punched him. But he knew that Leon would come round and that he would easily bend Leon to his will. Just the threat of one more punch would be enough. Ariston and Lysander were different. They looked like they might be harder nuts to crack. Leobotas decided, nonetheless, that he would crack them - whatever it took.

But there was worse to come for Leobotas.

"You must be punished, Leobotas," Nikandros continued. "You have put yourself forward without your pack's full support. It is your first day so I will not send you to the *ephors* for punishment. I will punish you myself."

Leobotas couldn't believe what he was hearing. This was all the fault of Ariston and Lysander and he swore to himself that he would make them pay for his punishment.

"Form a line, cubs," Nikandros declared. "Leobotas, I want you at the back. *Helots* bring forward the equipment."

The *helots* wheeled the little cart forward. It did not seem to contain much more than a pile of cloaks.

"Throughout your time in the *paides*," Nikandros explained. "You will only ever carry two pieces of equipment. You will never wear sandals or any other form of footwear. You will wear no clothes other than this cloak."

With that, Nikandros called each boy forward and gave them a bright red cloak from the hand cart. The cloak was big so that when each wrapped it around themselves it covered their entire body. The cloak was pinned at the shoulder with a single pin.

The second piece of equipment was a small sickle shaped knife called a *xyele* that was sharp on the inner curved edge and blunt on the outer curve.

"You will use the *xyele* for everything," Nikandros explained. "For cutting meat, preparing firewood, for fighting. Everything."

Lysander could feel that the cloak was made of a thick heavy material. He thought to himself that this would be too hot in the Spartan summer but not quite warm enough for the depths of a Spartan winter when the wind whipped through the Mani and sometimes snow lay on the ground. He felt the weight of the *xyele* and looked at its size. He thought this was too small with which to fight.

Eventually, the line got to Leobotas.

"Your punishment Leobotas is that you will not wear a red cloak. You will wear a blue cloak. This will mark you out to everybody as a bad leader and will bring shame on you and your family. You must continue to wear it until you have the support of all your pack or you have relinquished your claim to be leader."

"I have no father to shame," Leobotas replied defiantly. "And I don't care about my mother."

His cheeks were burning red with anger and Lysander felt this could only be a bad thing for him and Ariston.

IX

Back at Helen's house things were not going much better for her.

"Now," said Gorga. "I want you to show me that you are not just some silly little girl. I want you to run from here to the edge of Sparta, to where the river Eurotas forms a wide bed of reeds. Do you know this place?"

Helen knew exactly where Gorga was talking about. She had gone there often with her mother to have a picnic and bathe in the Eurotas while Pylos and Lampita had cut reeds from which to weave baskets or placed pots to catch the eels that swam in the reed beds.

She nodded. "That is a long way from here," she said. "It will take me one-and-a-half hours - at the very least."

Gorga smiled. "You have one hour," she said. "Otherwise, I will punish you."

"Are you coming with me to check?" asked Helen. "After all, I could just run to the edge of the village. Wait and then run back."

"No," replied Gorga. "I will wait here and I

will set up a gnomon to time you."

A gnomon was a stick stuck in the sand that Spartans used to mark the passage of time during the day. If they wanted to mark time after dark they lit a special candle with marks on it. But Helen and Gorga were talking in the heat of the day. If a gnomon was set up properly then the ground could be marked out into equal measures and when the gnomon's shadow moved from one line in the sand to the next, one hour had passed.

"Prepare yourself," said Gorga. "As soon as my gnomon is ready, you must run and return here before the marker reaches the next hour mark."

"How will you know if I have run all the way to the Eurotas?" asked Helen. She thought to herself that this was a clever question and it might, at least, force Gorga into coming with her. Helen thought that if she was going to have to run all that way it would make it easier if Gorga had to run, too. She wanted to see Gorga run because she was old and she didn't think Gorga would be very good at it.

"Good question, young lady," replied Gorga. "I will know that you have been to the Eurotas because you will bring me back a single reed from the river and you will collect a sample of the Eurotas's waters in this beaker."

With that Gorga handed Helen an earthenware beaker from under her *chiton* that she had been carrying all along but which Helen had not spotted.

"If you spill the water and the beaker is empty, you will need to run again. If you try to put water from elsewhere in the beaker I will know. I have drunk from the Eurotas all my life and I know its flavour like I know the taste of my own skin."

Helen's face crumpled. She had been defeated by Gorga and she knew she would have to run.

"My gnomon is almost ready," said Gorga. "Are you ready?"

Helen nodded.

"No, you are not," said Gorga. "Remove your sandals. You will run this race barefooted. We must toughen your feet as well as your legs."

Helen couldn't think of a way out of her predicament and so she reluctantly removed her sandals.

"Right, go!" shouted Gorga.

Helen set off at the fastest pace she could.

X

Nikandros looked hard at Leobotas and thought about whether to punish him further for his insolence. He decided on reflection that he would take it no further that day. He knew what was in store for the *paides* and he did not want to push Leobotas too far on his first day.

He took a step back and addressed his question to all the cubs. "Does anyone know where you will eat and sleep during your stay in the *agoge*?"

They all looked at him in a puzzled fashion. Eventually, Pausarius decided to guess. Lysander was slightly relieved to see that Pausarius had lost his nose streams. They seemed to have been smeared across his cheeks instead.

"Is there a building or a barn somewhere that will become our headquarters?"

Nikandros laughed at this reply.

"No," he said. "Your headquarters are here in this field. You will eat, sleep and train in this field. So you need to prepare it. First, you must sweep it, then you must dig a fire pit where these two *helots* will cook for you."

He turned and pointed at the two *helots* still standing by the cart.

"Finally, you must prepare your beds for the evening so that you can have your first night sleeping under the stars."

Lysander thought hard about what he was hearing. He had just left his lovely home with his kind, gentle mother and the two *helots* who did everything for him. Now he had hurt his hand and was going to have to sleep outside for the next five years at least... He fought hard to swallow a tear but his father's words came back to him. Rule number three echoed in his head - no self-pity. He took a deep breath and calmed himself.

"Here are your tools for this task," Nikandros

said.

The boys looked where he pointed and realised that the *helots* had taken away their old clothes without them noticing and had put in their place a whole pile of brooms and spades.

Leobotas jumped up quickly. He realised that he needed to show leadership and take command of the situation.

"Polydoros, Teleklos, Pausarius, Charillos and I will sweep the field so that it is clean and flat," he said. "Ariston, Lysander and Leon - you will dig our fire pit. Make it big because we will be hungry tonight after all this hard work."

Leobotas had quickly calculated that digging the fire pit was going to be harder work than sweeping the field and he gave that work to the three boys who had not supported him and who he blamed for having to wear the blue cloak.

XI

Helen ran as fast as she could to the Eurotas. She passed many houses and farms on the way and noticed all the *helots* at work in the gardens and the fields. There was the occasional woman or girl that she recognised and she waved to them as she sped past.

"Can't stop, I'm in training," she shouted proudly.

The people sometimes waved back and wished her well.

Helen quickly realised, however, the downside to running fast without sandals was that there were lots of little stones. These dug into her feet and made her hobble until she stopped and brushed them away. Every now and then one of the sharper stones would penetrate the skin on her feet making her jump and cry with pain until she picked it out with her nails. The wound would then fill with blood and her feet soon became a mess. The more she ran, the more bruised and cut her feet became. The bloodier her feet became the more the stones stuck to her feet in the wet blood.

Eventually, she learned to ignore the pain and just kept on running. She thought that if she kept stopping she wouldn't be able to get back in time and she wanted to prove Gorga wrong. She was not just a silly little girl.

After some time - she could not tell how long - she came around a corner and could see the banks of the Eurotas in the distance. She could see the reed beds clumped together and she headed for them first.

Arriving, she stopped to regain her breath for a second and then broke off a stem of the reeds, tucking it into her *chiton*. She then made her way to a stretch of the mighty river where it flowed more freely and she filled the beaker with water. Placing the beaker carefully on one side she waded into the river to clean her feet. The cold water felt good and she washed and bathed her soles until they looked better and didn't hurt so much.

Even though she had stopped she felt she had made good time and could still accomplish the task. She turned immediately and began the journey home.

The first thing she realised was that she couldn't run in the same way as she had before with the beaker full of water. She had only taken about thirty steps when she stood on a stone, jumped in pain and lost most of the water from the beaker. She ran quickly back to the river to refill it. She started to run back again but this time much more slowly. Picking her way carefully, looking down for stones all the time she concentrated on keeping every drop of water in the beaker. In truth, she moved little faster than a walking pace.

Eventually she arrived home and ran into the courtyard where she proudly placed the beaker of water at Gorga's feet and presented her with the broken reed.

"How did I do?" she gasped.

"You are late," said Gorga. "You have taken well past the hour mark. Look where the gnomon is pointing. You have failed completely. Just as I knew you would, you silly, pampered girl."

Helen was incredibly disappointed. She felt she had done well. The gnomon was only just past the hour mark. Her feet hurt but she felt she had accomplished the task and expected to be rewarded with some small treat as she was very hungry now.

"Drink the water from the beaker and go again," declared Gorga. "I will give you one-and-a-half hours this time as you are clearly not up to the original task."

"What!" demanded Helen. "You are not serious are you?"

"Go now," replied Gorga. "Go now or I will leave and tell your mother that she needs to find someone else for your training. This will bring great shame on your mother."

Helen felt she had no choice. She drank the water from the beaker and set off to run again.

XII

Lysander was pretty sure that he had broken his hand or at least badly damaged it. Digging the fire pit was agony and he wasn't really able to help much. Leon also did not seem up to the task. He couldn't breathe so well because the dried blood had formed a plug in both his nostrils making it difficult to inhale or exhale. It was really Ariston who did most of the work digging the pit but he didn't seem to mind. In fact, he seemed to relish being able to take his anger out on something and he dug with the strength of two boys.

Once the field was swept it started to look a little better. Although it didn't resemble home at least it looked clean. And once the fire pit was dug it looked even better. As soon as they had completed this task, Nikandros waved to the *helots* who brought in a metal frame to put over the fire and a couple of cooking pots so that they could cook the boys some food.

At that point Nikandros gathered the boys together and spoke to them. "You have made a good start. Your living and training area is looking like a proper camp. It is your job to clean it every day first thing when you get up. Do not get the *helots* to do that for you. It is part of your training and if ever I find your field unswept or untidy I will take you to the *ephors*. Do you all understand?"

The boys nodded.

"You will need some firewood for your cooking pit," Nikandros continued. "But first you must prepare your beds for tonight. You will do this by collecting reeds from the Eurotas and you will sleep on them. So, in order to have a good night's sleep you will need to collect a big bundle of reeds. Do any of you know how to get to the Eurotas from here?"

Every single boy raised his hand. The Eurotas was the life blood of Sparta. Its waters provided them with drinking and cooking water. Its wildlife provided them with both birds and fish for food and its reed beds provided them with bedding, basket making material and eels. It was also a great place to swim and most children would do this in the Eurotas every summer.

"Good," said Nikandros. "The only other thing is that you must leave your *xyele* here in the camp. It is tradition that on the first night the new cubs must collect their bedding with nothing more than their bare hands. You must break the reed stems with your hands and collect as many as you can."

At this point Lysander was really regretting hitting Leobotas. His hand was swelling up and ached like mad. The idea of having to collect reeds with only his bare hands filled him with dread. He tried hard to think about his father's rule three - no self-pity. So, he took a deep breath and steeled himself with a new sense of determination.

"Come, let's go," said Nikandros. "The Eurotas is a long way from here. So, let's get started."

And with that, the party of boys put their *xyeles* in a pile under an olive tree and set off one behind the other to walk to the river Eurotas.

In summer, Sparta was quite a dry and dusty land. It was very rocky and quite hilly, particularly as you approached the foothills of the Taygetos mountains. The agriculture was good in the valleys with many vegetable plots and fields of oats and wheat. There were many orchards and groves of trees rich with fruit. Away from the valley floor, however, the vegetation became more sparse and the landscape was punctuated only with the odd tree or grove.

The most common tree in Sparta was the olive tree. This was lucky as the olives that grew on them were also tasty and provided food for the Spartans. There were fig, orange and lemon trees in the areas where there was farming as these also provided food.

In the foothills there were other, less familiar kinds of trees. Most of these were unknown to Lysander but he did know two; the salix and the cork tree. The cork tree provided a kind of soft spongy wood that the Spartans used for lots of things around the home. The salix tree was rather special. Lysander's mother had shown him that if you stripped a small piece of the bark, soaked it in water and then sucked on it, it would help to ease pain a little.

About an hour into their walk Lysander's eyes widened. Just off the path, up ahead he could see a large salix tree and there were some patches on the tree where the bark had begun to peel. He suspected someone else had been sampling its medicinal properties. He took a few quick steps off the path, grabbed as many pieces of bark as he could and shoved one of them into his mouth.

As he approached the tree he also spotted a bee hive on the tree behind, high up in the branches. He didn't really think much about it at the time because of his pain. It did remind him, however, that he liked honey and that he was hungry.

XIII

Helen was extremely tired by now. She had run all the way back to the Eurotas without any food and only a single beaker of water to drink. Her feet were getting badly cut again and she was thinking all the time how Gorga was being incredibly mean to her and that she would complain to her mother tonight.

She managed to make it to the Eurotas again and went through the same routine of breaking off a single reed, filling the beaker and bathing her injured feet. She did it quicker this time though as she knew it was the length of time it had taken her to bathe her feet and then make the return journey that had cost her.

A cunning plan was brewing. Last time when she had run with the beaker full of water she had just held it out in her hand and moved slower so as not to spill any. This meant that she was barely able to run at a pace faster than walking. This time she decided that she would cover the top of the beaker with her spare hand so as not to spill the water.

This would mean that she should be able to return much faster and get back within the hour. She was looking forward to doing this so much because she felt sure that Gorga would reward her with a cool drink of water, some snacks and a rest.

Filling the beaker, her theory was put to the test. She smiled to herself because it seemed to work. Helen felt good. She felt that her plan was a good one and that she was making a fast time. She put her head down and really started to run as fast as she could for the last leg of the journey. Nothing could stop her and she would soon be done with this stupid exercise.

Just over half-way back Helen noticed a small troop of boys in the far distance coming towards her. They were all dressed in red cloaks except one who wore a blue one. She didn't know what this meant but she knew it was a mark that that person had done something wrong. The boys all looked about Lysander's age and she wondered whether he could be among them.

Helen was too far away to tell at the start but as she ran towards them, she began to get a better view of their faces. She saw one boy peel away from the group briefly to pull at a tree. As the boy turned, she recognised him - it was Lysander! In her excitement, she forgot herself and lifted her hand from the top of the beaker to wave, and shouted, "Hello." At that very moment, just as she lifted her hand, she trod on a particularly sharp stone. It broke the skin of her foot again and she jumped up in agony. In the process, she dropped the beaker and its contents leaked into the soil. She couldn't believe it and looked in horror and astonishment at the empty beaker lying on its side.

Lysander didn't even notice her and the troop of boys passed by her in the distance with their heads bent downwards. She lay on her stomach staring at the beaker for some time trying to work out what to do.

In the end, she stood up, dusted herself off and ran back to the Eurotas. She filled the beaker and ran back to Gorga. She had tears in her eyes for some of the way but she couldn't wipe them, of course, because she had two hands on the beaker.

Gorga was waiting for her in the courtyard again. Helen was utterly exhausted. She handed the full beaker to Gorga who looked at her sternly.

"You took nearly two hours this time. What is wrong with you? You stupid girl. Are you just not interested in trying?" asked Gorga.

Helen couldn't help it. She blurted out exactly what had happened and explained that she had had to go back to the river to refill the beaker.

"Well, that, at least, is admirable," said Gorga. "At least you went back to fill the beaker. Some would have returned with it empty as you had gone more than half- way. But you have still not completed my task. I will give you thirty minutes to rest. You may have some honey and nuts and plenty of water. But then you must run again."

Helen was so tired she didn't even have the energy to protest. She just sat disconsolately while the *helots* brought her refreshments and she mentally prepared herself to complete the task a third time.

XIV

The salix bark slowly started to have a slight effect. Lysander's hand started to ache less than it had done before. But it still ached a lot and they were at the reed bed too quickly for the salix to have any strong impact.

Nikandros led the way to the reed beds and instructed them to collect as many reeds as they could carry. He explained that they would have one hour to collect as many as possible. Furthermore, he explained again that the reeds would form their beds, so the more they could collect the more comfortable their sleep would be.

The boys started their arduous task. Wading into the shallow banks of the Eurotas they knelt down in the water and were able to break the stems of the reeds below the water line. It required quite a lot of pressure but eventually each reed stem would snap with a loud crack.

Of course, Lysander struggled. He worked out a way of holding the reed with his good hand and snapping the stem with his feet. It worked but it was slow. As a result, Lysander's bundle of reeds was much smaller than anyone else's. Both Ariston and Leon tried to help him a little by giving him a few of their own reeds but as soon as Leobotas spotted this he stopped them and shouted that Nikandros had told each of them to collect their own. He came over to Lysander and took the reeds that Ariston and Leon had given him and smashed them to pieces in front of Lysander. He then returned to the task of collecting his own reeds.

It was with a heavy heart that Lysander trudged back to camp with the other boys. He knew he was in for an uncomfortable night's sleep. His bed would not be soft enough and his hand would be throbbing.

At least I will get some food, he thought. "I am really hungry after all that has happened."

Nikandros pointed to a spot underneath a group of olive trees. "Make your beds there cubs, under the shade of the olives. Do not sleep so close that you wake each other but do not sleep so far apart that you cannot come to each other's aid if it is needed. There are still wolves in Sparta and you never know when the Persians might attack."

Nikandros disappeared while the boys made their beds. Most of the boys knew that Nikandros was teasing them. Wolves had not been seen in Sparta for many years. Wolves were still around and could be found in some of the wilder places, particularly the Taygetos mountains, but they were unlikely to come down to the edge of town. Leon, however, was not very worldly and he looked distinctly uncomfortable about the fact that wolves or even Persians might arrive.

As a result, he tried to build his bed in between as many of the other boys as he could.

When Nikandros came back the boys had all made their beds and were standing next to them waiting for Nikandros to inspect them. But Nikandros was not alone. He had brought another teenager with him.

"This is Agis," he explained. "He is a *paidiskoi* who is training another group of cubs. I have asked him to inspect your beds because I am your *paidiskoi* and I might show you favour. Spartan tradition requires rigorous fairness at all costs. So, Agis will make the judgement for me."

Agis started to walk among the rows of beds that the boys had constructed. He could be heard to mutter, "...passable," under his breath as he went past each bed in turn. When he got to Lysander's, he stopped. He gave the thin mat of reeds a good kick and sent them scattering everywhere.

"This bed is not adequate," he said. "This bed brings shame on the whole cub pack."

Agis then left to tend to his own charges. Nikandros watched him go. When Agis had left, Nikandros turned to the boys. "You heard the judgement of Agis. Lysander's bed is not adequate. This brings shame on the whole pack and so you must be punished as a group. My decision is that the *helots* will not make you any food tonight. You will go hungry and you will all feel the shame of your failure in your empty stomachs. Now, drink some water, get yourselves ready for bed and sleep well. We have a full day tomorrow and I will return just before sunrise."

The boys could not believe what they were hearing. After all that had happened today they had to go to bed without any food. Leobotas blamed Lysander and started to make loud threatening noises about what he was going to do to Lysander tomorrow.

XV

Helen returned from the Eurotas for a third time. She was utterly exhausted and had already decided that if Gorga made her run again, she would refuse. She was expecting to be told to run again because she knew that her time had been longer than before. She knew that if she refused to run this would mean that Gorga would no longer be her trainer and that this would bring shame on her and her mother. But she didn't care. She was just so tired.

She handed the beaker to Gorga with the water still in it. Her head was bowed down and she expected to hear harsh words and to be told to run again. She prepared herself to rebel.

Instead, Gorga spoke to her a little more

softly, "I am impressed," she said. "You have done all that I told you. No-one has ever made that journey in under an hour. It is impossible - but you came close on your first attempt. We may be able to make a fine Spartan woman out of you after all."

Helen could not believe what she had just heard - *it was impossible to run to the Eurotas and back in under an hour* - and yet she had nearly done it. Helen felt a mixture of stupidity for being tricked like that by Gorga and pride for actually achieving what she had done.

"Go to bed now, Helen," Gorga said. "I will be back in the morning and we will have another heavy day ahead of us."

Helen nodded wearily and headed to her room for a good night's sleep.

XVI

Helen's and Lysander's thoughts in their separate beds were very different that night.

Helen went to sleep quickly because she was shattered. She did not exactly like Gorga - after all, she had been mean to her - but she did begin to respect her a little and thought that her training might actually be worth it.

In contrast Lysander lay awake for a long time. His hand still throbbed, his bed was uncomfortable and he kept turning over the events of the day in his mind. His father's three rules kept coming back to him. Make friends with the other boys - well that hadn't happened. They all hated him except for Ariston and Leon. Don't put yourself first - well that hadn't happened either. Lysander had put his friendship with Ariston first and as a result he had made an enemy of Leobotas and all the other boys who supported Leobotas. Never have self-pity - well that wasn't quite working either. Lysander was definitely feeling sorry for himself. He wrapped his cloak tightly around himself, made the best of the thin bed he was on and made a pledge to himself that tomorrow was going to be a better day. He fell asleep at that thought.

CHAPTER III
Day Two in the agoge

I

Nikandros was as good as his word. He arrived early in the morning before dawn and woke the boys from their sleep.

"Good morning, *paides*," he said. "It's a new day and we have much to do. Rise and get prepared. I want to brief you around the campfire in a few moments."

With that, he went over to the *helots* and gave them instructions to light a fire and prepare things for the *paides*.

After a while all the boys had risen, removed the sleep from their eyes and fastened their cloaks around them. They were all hungry and still tired from their first night sleeping under the stars. The only one that didn't seem to mind was Pausarius. Lysander guessed that this was not the first time that Pausarius had gone hungry nor the first night that he had slept under the stars.

The boys started to gather and to sit around the fire that the *helots* were making. It didn't give off much heat yet but there was still something comforting about being wrapped in a thick cloak and sitting in front of a fire with flames licking high.

Nikandros started to brief them about the day. "Firstly, you will have some breakfast. The *helots* will prepare it for you. It will not be a feast but it will give you some energy. Whether you are fed again today will depend entirely on how you do during the day. If I feel that any one of you is not trying to the best of their ability I will punish that boy by giving him no food tonight. If Leobotas is still wearing a blue cloak by the end of today I will punish all of you with no food."

Leobotas visibly snarled at this and he shot a filthy glance at Lysander and Ariston. He mouthed something at them. They couldn't make out the words but they guessed it was not something pleasant.

"You do not need to stick with Leobotas as your leader," Nikandros continued. "But you must elect a leader that has the support of all of you."

Polydoros and Teleklos moved closer to Leobotas and put their hands on his shoulder so as to signal their continued loyalty. Leobotas remained unmoved and just continued to stare at Lysander and Ariston.

"Does anyone have any questions at this stage?" asked Nikandros.

Charillos shuffled a little uneasily in his seat. "What is for breakfast?" he asked.

Nikandros smiled. "Good question. Your breakfast this morning will be the same as your breakfast every single day during your time in the *paides*. It is the finest breakfast that can be had in the whole of Sparta. It will nourish you and help you to build bones and muscle."

Charillos started to visibly lick his lips. He and some of the other boys started to imagine a hearty breakfast of pork meat, eggs, cornbread and honey. This was one of Charillos's favourite meals and he couldn't wait to wolf it down.

"You will each have a portion of pig's blood porridge," Nikandros explained. "The *helots* will pour some pig's blood into the pan and they will stir in some oats and cook them together to make the porridge. Once you have tasted it you will thank all the Gods for the fact that you have been born in Sparta."

Charillos's face visibly crumpled. It was plain that the idea of pig's blood porridge was not one that appealed to him.

"I must speak to Agis," said Nikandros. "I will return in a little while when the porridge is ready. We will talk further then."

II

Once he had finished speaking, Nikandros got up and left the camp. All went silent for a little while. Then Leobotas got up and pointed at Lysander and Ariston.

"You two. I want a word with you," he said. "In private."

He gestured to an area under the olive trees a little way distant from the rest of the camp.

"Let's speak there."

He started to walk to the place he had identified.

Lysander shot Ariston a puzzled glance. Neither were sure what to do but both decided that it would be best if they joined Leobotas together and listened to what he had to say.

When they got to the quiet spot away from the rest of the camp, Leobotas spoke to them in a low menacing voice. It was almost as though he was spitting the words out rather than speaking them.

"You two are the reason we were all hungry last night. I don't intend to go hungry again tonight. You will support me today otherwise I will deliver some punishment of my own. My punishment will hurt a lot more than just being hungry. Do you both understand me?"

Both Lysander and Ariston said nothing in reply. They both just looked concerned and a little frightened. It was clear to them that Leobotas did not intend to gain their support by showing them his leadership qualities or by getting them on side. He was going to bully them into it.

Lysander understood immediately why this offended his sense of fairness. Leobotas was breaking his father's second rule. He was putting himself and his own interests before the interests of the group. He quickly made up his mind that he would not support Leobotas while he continued to act like a bully.

Eventually, Lysander spoke first. "If you can show yourself to be a good leader today and your decisions are taken with the good of the whole pack in mind then I will support you."

Ariston nodded his head in agreement.

"I see you both intend to defy me further," Leobotas hissed. "In that case, we will see who comes off worst at the end of the day."

III

At that moment Nikandros returned to the camp and so Leobotas returned to the fire pit. Lysander and Ariston were relieved as they felt Leobotas had just been about to hit them. The boys sat down in a circle around Nikandros. The *helots* handed each of them a small bowl with a portion of pigs blood porridge in the bottom.

It is hard to describe pigs blood porridge if you have not seen it before. The pig's blood is mixed with a little water to stop it forming a clot when it is heated. Nonetheless, it thickens considerably and turns almost black in colour. The oats are added and cooked in the pigs blood so that they too get coated in a thick black mess. The overall effect is one of having a mass of black lumpy stuff in the bottom of your bowl. So, the look of the food was not good. The taste was even worse. It was thick and cloying. It stuck to your teeth and the roof of your mouth. You had to physically swallow hard to make it go down your throat and it had a strange but really strong taste of iron that made it even more difficult to swallow.

Lysander looked around the group of boys to see who was enjoying the food. He saw that all of them were hesitating to eat the porridge. The only ones who were eating it were Pausarius and Leobotas. Lysander guessed that this was because Pausarius had eaten pigs blood porridge before and was used to the taste and that Leobotas was eating it to prove that he was leadership material.

Lysander thought about all of this and at that very moment his stomach rumbled. He realised he hadn't eaten for over a day and that he was hungry. He decided to put aside his distaste of the food and get on with eating it. He slowly started to eat the porridge spoonful by spoonful. The other boys started to follow suit and soon they were all tucking in.

"Good," said Nikandros. "Eat up boys for we have a full day ahead of us. Also, I have some important news for you."

The boys waited to hear the news.

"Today we will concentrate on athletics," Nikandros explained. "We will go to the training academy and we will start your education in each of the disciplines. This is important because there is to be a festival in one month's time. We will compete against the other cub packs and some girls from the *gymnasium* will be invited to compete, too. This is an opportunity for the whole of Sparta to see the new intake to the *agoge* and lots of people will attend. So, we have one month to get you into shape and to win that competition. Eat up and we will make our way to the training ground."

The boys were instantly excited. They knew this festival because most of them had attended as spectators when they were younger. It was called the *gymnopaedia* or *festival of young athletes* and it was one of the three most important festivals in the Spartan calendar. They knew it was a big event and now they were going to be taking part. The camp started to buzz with excitement.

IV

Helen was woken by her mother who told her that Gorga would be here soon and that she should get dressed and have breakfast before Gorga arrived. Helen did as she was asked and waited for the *helots* to bring her meal. She watched Pylos as he entered her room with a bowl of cereal and expected him to do what he usually did - to lay it on the table, to bow to her and then to leave the room. But this morning Pylos didn't do that. He laid the bowl on the table but then he turned to Helen.

"Mistress Helen," he said. "May I speak with you please?"

Helen was so shocked that she quickly nodded yes. Normally, this would be an extraordinary thing for a *helot* to do - to speak to a Spartan without being asked to speak first. But there was something in Pylos's manner which told her this was important and that she should agree to break the normal rules just for once.

"I am worried about Lysander," said Pylos. "I spoke to my mother about what he will face in the *agoge*. She told me that on the first few days he is likely to be lonely and hungry. The trainers use hunger as a way to test the boys' strength of character and will."

Helen had two reactions to this news from Pylos. Firstly, she was worried about Lysander. When she had seen him briefly yesterday he had looked gaunt and in pain. Secondly, she wondered why Pylos was speaking to her about this. The latter question was the one that came out first.

"Why are you telling me this?" she asked.

Pylos wanted to tell her it was because Lysander was kind to him and he considered him to be his friend in a world where he had no other friends. But he knew that would be a death sentence for both him and Lysander. Friendships between Spartans and *helots* were forbidden and could be punishable by beating or even death. So, instead, he replied in a way that was designed to throw Helen off the scent.

"Lysander is your brother," he said. "I know that you love him dearly. So, I thought you would want to know about it as I know you are a kind mistress and you will want to do something to help your brother."

Helen thought about this for a moment. She recognised that Pylos had given her a clever answer and had turned things back onto her. Nonetheless, she was intrigued.

"What can we do about it?" she asked.

"Well, Mistress," replied Pylos. "You could send me on an errand this morning that will take me out of the house. You could tell me to collect a big basket of eggs from the chicken runs and I could go to Lysander's training ground. I could leave him some biscuits and a few eggs - not so many that anyone would notice - and I could leave him a note from you with the eggs and biscuits."

Helen thought about this.

"But I don't know where his training ground is," she replied. "It is a secret."

"Mistress Gorga will know," said Pylos. "She knows everything."

Helen fell silent. She thought some more about this. She made a pretence of disliking her brother but really she loved him deeply and did not like the idea of him being hungry and suffering. So, eventually she nodded to Pylos.

"I will see what I can find out," she said.

V

Gorga arrived shortly afterwards. She greeted Helen.

"I have some good news for you. You did well yesterday. I was pleased with you. As a reward, we will spend this morning doing mathematics and then this afternoon we will practise singing. This day will help your legs to rest after all your running so that we can start tomorrow to continue to build up your legs. How does that sound?"

Helen wanted to immediately blurt out the question that was uppermost in her mind, *do you know where Lysander's training camp is?* But she knew that would be suspicious. So, instead, she replied with a different question.

"Mathematics? What is the point of that?"

Gorga sighed. The young girls that she trained always asked the same question - what is the point of mathematics?

Gorga knew that if Helen was like all the other girls she had trained, then her answer would be unlikely to convince Helen and she would have a difficult morning ahead of her. Gorga thought carefully about how to explain things.

"Life is not all just about running, jumping, singing and dancing you know. As a Spartan woman you will have great responsibilities. If you want to build a new house for yourself, how will you know how much timber to order, how many roof tiles to collect, what shape to build the house? Mathematics will enable you to work out the answers to all these questions."

Helen thought about this. She could see this actually made sense.

"If you have a great journey to go on," Gorga continued. "How will you know how to calculate the amount of time it will take and the provisions that you will need to sustain you along the way?"

Helen nodded. She could see that this would be helpful.

"Can we start with distances?" she asked.

Gorga quickly nodded her approval. She was pleased with the new interest that Helen was showing for the subject and Gorga congratulated herself on her ability to inspire her new pupil.

"If I wanted to set out now to see the boys training in this year's *agoge*," asked Helen, "how would I calculate how long it would take me to get to their academy? I know that I am not allowed to do that but I thought it might be a good use of mathematics."

"Oh, you wouldn't go to an academy," said Gorga immediately. "You would go to Mentos Field."

Gorga quickly regretted saying this. She knew, exactly as Helen had said, that families were not supposed to see their boys for at least one month after they entered the *agoge*. She became suspicious that Helen might be trying to trick her.

She paused and thought about it for a moment. Eventually, she decided that it didn't matter because she would be with Helen all day and she would keep a close eye on her.

In order to prevent Gorga thinking further about things, Helen quickly asked for help, "please, show me how you would calculate how much time we would need to get to Mentos Field. I know I don't need to go there but I would like to know how mathematics can answer that question."

Helen was doing a good job of throwing Gorga off the scent.

"Well, we would need to know the precise distance in paces from here to the fields," Gorga replied. "Then we would need to know your average walking pace. We would then divide the first number by the second number and that would tell us the amount of time needed to get there. Do you know how to do division?"

Helen shook her head. She had got all the information she needed. She didn't need to ask how far it was to Mentos field because she knew that Pylos would know exactly where it was. So, she was now happy to go along with Gorga's plan to do mathematics. She just needed to find a way to get the information to Pylos.

So, Gorga and Helen settled down for the rest of the morning to do division, multiplication, addition and subtraction. Helen found that she even enjoyed solving some of the problems.

Gorga had a small bag with lots of wooden boards for writing on and they did the mathematics on these. The boards could be wiped clean afterwards. But Helen also noticed that Gorga had some small sheets of parchment - a kind of paper - in her bag. When Gorga took a break to go to the toilet she took a small piece of parchment from Gorga's bag and wrote, "Mentos Field" on it.

Mid-morning Pylos brought them both some refreshments. A beaker of cold milk each and a plate of figs. When she had finished the figs Helen secretly used the milk to wet the bottom of the plate. When Gorga was writing another difficult calculation for her to perform she stuck the piece of parchment to the bottom of the plate.

She then called for Pylos to come and clear away the empty refreshments. When he came into the room she gave him a quick wink with one eye - on the side that Gorga couldn't see - and she quickly looked down at her plate. To distract Gorga even further, Helen quickly turned to her. "That calculation looks too difficult for me. Please can you show me how to do it again?"

Gorga smiled that she had posed such a difficult question that it had made Helen ask for help. She felt that she was beginning to get Helen to be more obedient and so she kindly obliged.

As Pylos collected the dishes, he piled them in one hand and the beakers in the other. As soon as Helen's plate touched his hand he felt the piece of parchment underneath and guessed that was why Helen had winked at him. As he left the room he removed the parchment and read "Mentos Field". He carefully folded the parchment and put it into his tunic.

Now, in fact, Helen had not been as clever as she thought. She had not considered the fact that most *helots* could not read. The Spartans deliberately kept the helots uneducated so that they could not pass notes and the like between themselves. But in this case, Helen was incredibly lucky. Lampita, Pylos's mother, felt it was important that Pylos knew how to read and write and most evenings after the Spartans had settled down for bed, Lampita would spend time showing Pylos how to read by the light of a little reed lamp. It did not give off much light and it only lasted a short while but it was enough, over time, for Pylos to be able to read and write to a basic standard.

So, he knew instantly what Helen's note said and where he must go.

VI

The boys were all excited to enter the training ground.

"We are going to start with the long jump," Nikandros said. "First let me show you how to do it."

He took the boys over to a pit of sand that was in one corner of the stadium. Then he picked up two lead weights that had leather straps attached to their tops and slid each hand into a strap.

"You run from here," he explained. "You leap from this wooden strip here. You throw the weights forward in front of you until you are near the point where you think you are going to land. At that point, you throw the weights behind you to get an extra bit of distance."

And with that, Nikandros launched himself into a jump. He was clearly practised in this event and good at it. His run up was effortless. He used the weights perfectly to give himself extra distance. He released them at just the right time and he landed in the sand, almost standing.

"Who thinks they can beat that?" he asked. "The boy who makes the furthest mark from the starting point will be the winner. Who is first up? What about you Lysander?"

Lysander took the weights from Nikandros and slipped his hands into the straps. He had expected it to hurt his still bruised hand but to his surprise he found it didn't. Perhaps he hadn't broken his hand after all. Perhaps he had just bruised it.

He took a deep breath, commenced his run up and went as fast as he could. He tried to take off as close to the wooden strip as he could and he flung his arms forward with the weights. He felt the sensation of being pulled through the air and enjoyed it. In fact, he enjoyed it so much that he forgot to let go of the weights and so he landed in the sand with them still in his hands.

"Don't forget to release the weights next time," said Nikandros. "You will each have three jumps and your longest jump will be the one that counts."

So, each of the boys took it in turn. This was an event that suited boys with strong legs and light frames. Although Lysander got the hang of letting go of the weights on his next two jumps, it was Polydoros who was the natural. Polydoros was lean, well muscled and quite tall. All of these qualities helped him to be a strong performer at the long jump and he beat Lysander by a good margin in the end. Lysander was second, followed by Ariston, Teleklos, Leobotas, Pausarius, Leon and Charillos. Leon was smaller than average size and Charillos was a little heavier than most so they were both at a disadvantage.

VII

Next was the discus. This was a round flat circle of wood edged with a ring of bronze all the way round. The discus had been used as a weapon in Greece's ancient past when the metal disc was sharpened so that it had an edge. These days, however, it had been replaced as a throwing weapon by the javelin and was used just for sport. So, the metal disc was blunt. But the discus could still cause a nasty injury if it hit you on the head. Nikandros started again by showing the boys what to do.

"You start like this," he said. "With your arms out straight. You hold the discus in your right hand with your hand on top. You stand feet apart facing the opposite direction in which you wish to throw. You then spin around quickly, one-and-a-half times, going as fast as you can and then when you are facing the direction that you want to throw, you release the discus and see how far it flies."

And with that Nikandros did exactly as he had described. Spinning around at a ferocious rate he released the discus at the end of his spin and gave a grunt with the effort of putting all his power into giving the discus as much force as he could.

The boys watched with awe as the disc sailed into the air, spinning around with perfect balance and flying through the air. It travelled a good forty paces and bounced in the sand at the end.

"Who's first?" asked Nikandros. "Charillos, what about you? I think that you may like this event."

Charillos happily stepped forward and took a fresh discus from Nikandros. He assumed the same position that Nikandros had taken and he tried to copy the identical spinning motion. Unfortunately, however, he got a little dizzy and tripped as he tried to complete his spin. This meant that he fell over just at the point when he released the discus. Instead of flying high into the air it came low and flat across the ground to where the other boys were standing. They had to take evasive action. Fortunately, the discus was not travelling fast and so they were easily able to avoid it.

"Never mind, Charillos," said Nikandros. "You will have three goes in total so you can get it right next time."

The other boys each came up and had a go. Ariston was quite good at this but again, Leon was a little too small to be able to put much force into it.

Then it came to Leobotas' turn. He assumed the position and quickly out of the corner of his eye he glanced at Lysander to make sure he could see exactly where he was standing. He did his one-and-a-half spins and just like Charillos had done, he tripped at the end and released the discus in the wrong direction. This time, however, it wasn't moving slowly. It was moving fast. Very fast. And it was headed directly towards Lysander's head. It took a fraction of a second for Lysander to realise what was happening but just in time he turned his head away and raised his shoulder to try to protect himself. It was exactly the right thing to do as the discus thudded into Lysander's shoulder with such a force that it nearly knocked him off his feet. The pain was sharp and shot down his arm.

"Unlucky, Leobotas," said Nikandros. "You will have two more turns to get it right. Lysander are you all right?"

It was clear that Nikandros thought this was an accident. But Lysander was clear that it was not. Leobotas was looking at him with a snarl on his lips and a dark look in his eyes. Lysander was clear that this had been an attempt by Leobotas to really injure him. He knew that if the discus had hit his head rather than his shoulder he would be lying on the ground right now, seriously injured. Despite feeling that he had had a close shave he nodded to Nikandros that he was fine.

Lysander's suspicions were further reinforced during the next two rounds of this competition. For throws two and three Leobotas was able to throw the discus perfectly well. In fact, because he was a big strong boy, it turned out that this was Leobotas's event and he won it easily.

VIII

Pylos was able to slip away after the lunch dishes had been cleaned away and all the tasks for the afternoon had been completed. He knew exactly where to go and he headed straight for Mentos Field. He stopped only to fill a basket with eggs and a few biscuits and cover it with a small cloth. When he got near to Mentos Field he started to move more slowly and to stick to the shadows under the olive trees and any patches of long grass. His heart was pounding as he did not want to be seen. He knew that at any moment he could fall victim to one of the *krupteia*.

The *krupteia* were Spartan boys who had finished the *agoge* at the age of eighteen but who had not yet joined the army. They were required to live outside the city and live only on their own wits for one year. They had to steal and forage for their own food and had not to be seen in the daytime. At night they were allowed to roam around freely and it was the law that if they found a *helot* away from his or her master then the *krupteia* could legally murder the *helot*.

It was daytime so the *krupteia* should not be around but Pylos could not be absolutely certain. He was scared and saw movement in every shadow. As he approached the field itself he had expected to see the boys training and to see activity going on. He was confused, however, as he could see no-one. There was no activity at all. He could see the little beds made of reeds but he could see no people at all and certainly no boys. He stood there looking confused and didn't know what to do. Eventually, he caught sight of a small movement under one of the trees. It was a person stirring from sleep. He looked closer and realised that there were two people under the trees. They were hardly moving but they were dressed in the clothing of *helots*. In particular, he could see the dog caps on their heads. This was a cap literally made from a dog that Spartans sometimes made *helots* wear to remind them that they were no better than animals. Pylos guessed that these might be the *helots* assigned to work for the *agoge*. He could not rule out the possibility that they might be *krupteia* in disguise but he reassured himself with the thought that they were unlikely to be together. *Krupteia* usually moved alone. He quickly made his way towards the figures and spoke to them in the Messenian dialect.

"Do either of you know which bed is that of Lysander?"

"Why do you ask?" replied one of the *helots* with a perfect Messenian accent.

"His sister has asked me to bring him some eggs as a gift," replied Pylos. "I want to leave them in his bed."

"But that's not allowed," replied the *helot*. "We could all get into trouble if you do that."

Pylos thought for a moment and then replied, "I have orders from his sister. I am only a *helot* and I cannot refuse to complete an order. If you are concerned for your safety then you should leave to get some water and give me a few moments alone here. In that way, you will not see what I have done and you cannot be held responsible."

The two *helots* agreed and left to find some water for the evening's cooking. Before they left, one of the *helots* pointed to Lysander's bed.

"It is that one," he said. "He is injured, too."

When they were gone Pylos placed six eggs and a few biscuits carefully in Lysander's bed and covered them with reeds so that they were padded and could not be seen. He took Helen's handwritten scrap of parchment and tucked that into the reed bed also with just a tiny corner sticking out. He hoped that Lysander would see it and that he would recognise Helen's scrawl.

After that he left and quickly returned to Lysander's house. He was relieved to get home safely. On the way home he reflected how grateful he was that Mistress Demetria did not make him or his mother wear a dog cap.

IX

Back in the training ground, Nikandros decided

it was time to test how good the boys were at running. He explained what was involved in the running races. "You will run two races. The first is called the *stade*. It is exactly two hundred paces in length across the length of the training ground. You will all set off at the same time and the winner will be the one who crosses the finish line first."

The boys nodded. This didn't sound too difficult and they were relieved to hear that this was the next test.

Nikandros continued his explanation. "The *stade* is designed to test how fast you are over a short distance. This is about how quickly you can close with the enemy once you have both taken to the field of battle."

The boys nodded again.

"After that," continued Nikandros. "You will have a short rest and then we will run the *dolichos*. This will be ten laps of the training ground. The *dolichos* is designed to test your stamina over a long distance. This is about how quickly you can cover the distance from your camp to where the enemy is trying to get to. If you can get there before them you will have an advantage. There is another race, the *diaulos,* a middle distance race but we will not run that today."

All the boys felt less positive about this race. Except Leon. Leon enjoyed running long distances and he often ran around Sparta for enjoyment. He found that it cleared his mind and made him feel good afterwards.

X

The *stade* was a quick affair. They all put their full energy into exploding down the track as fast as they could. Although they ran barefoot, the training ground was well swept and there were no stones so they could go at full speed. The *stade* favoured those boys who were tall and lean with strong leg muscles. It was a close run thing between Ariston, Lysander and Polydoros but Ariston just managed to get across the line first with Polydoros next and Lysander a close third. It was easy to predict but Charillos came last as he was clearly not built as a runner. Just in front of him was Pausarius, who was a little too skinny. Leon was next and then Leobotas was in the middle.

Nikandros was as good as his word. He gave them a short rest and then lined them up for the *dolichos*.

Lysander started well in this race and went flying off into an early lead but soon realised that it was not possible to go at full speed for all this distance and so he began to tire after a couple of laps. Leon had felt confident before the race and his confidence proved to be well founded. Because he was small but quite light he was able to keep up a good pace for every lap of the race. In fact, so good was his running technique that he did his tenth lap while all the other boys were on their ninth and Charillos was on his eighth.

Lysander noted to himself that a different boy had so far won each event and he began to realise that this was because each boy had different strengths. He thought that if ever he could become leader of the group he would use this insight to work out how best to use each of the different members of the pack.

Leobotas had no such thoughts. The only thing on his mind was how he could punish Ariston. He had already managed to hurt Lysander and he was confident that this had taught him a lesson. He noticed how Lysander avoided his gaze when he looked at him and this told him that Lysander was scared of him and would not dare to challenge him any more. Now he needed to punish Ariston and he felt confident that this would then force them both into supporting him this evening so that he could lose the hated blue cloak.

XI

It would not be long before Leobotas got his chance.

Nikandros explained that the next event would be the shot put. The boys had to throw a heavy round weight into the air for the furthest distance possible. They had to take it in turns and throw from behind the same line. Again, Nikandros demonstrated the technique. Facing the opposite direction in which he wanted to throw, he tucked the shot put into his neck and then did a half spin and lift until he was facing the correct direction. At which point he launched the shot put as far as he could. Again, it travelled a good distance. Nikandros asked the boys to line up to take it in turns. In front of Leobotas was Charillos and behind him was Ariston. This meant that Charillos went first. Everyone expected Charillos to put in his usual performance. Either to be clumsy and fall over or to throw it a really short distance. But this time Charillos did not do as everyone expected. He took the shot. He noted how heavy it felt in his hand. He did his half spin perfectly and launched it into the air with a huge grunt. To everyone's amazement the shot put sailed through the air and went almost as far as Nikandros had thrown it. Everyone stood open-mouthed for a moment.

"Well done, Charillos. Fantastic throw," applauded Nikandros. "Now go get it back and hand it to Leobotas."

Charillos did as he was asked and handed the shot put to Leobotas, who made a pretence that Charillos had passed it to him so badly that it had caused him to drop it. It was not true though. Charillos had not passed it badly. Leobotas dropped it on purpose and he did it because he directed the drop so that the shot put landed directly on Ariston's foot. Ariston gave a short cry and then began hopping about in pain while holding his foot. After a little while Nikandros was able to stop him hopping so that he could take a look at his foot. It was clear immediately that Ariston would play no further part in the training that day. Two of his toes had been badly crushed. He had lost the nail on one and the other was already swelling badly.

Leobotas started proclaiming loudly that it was an "accident" and that "he hadn't meant to do it", "it wasn't on purpose." No-one believed him. Not even Nikandros.

Lysander offered to miss the rest of the shot put so that he could attend to Ariston's foot. Nikandros agreed to this and so Lysander took Ariston to one side. He asked the *helots* to give him a bowl of water to bathe Ariston's foot and a strip of cloth so that he could bandage it. He had also kept some of the salix bark in his loin cloth and he offered a piece to Ariston for him to chew. Once Lysander had washed away the blood, applied a bandage to Ariston's foot and the effect of the salix bark started to work, Ariston began to feel a little better.

The shot put competition ended by the time Lysander finished tending to Aritson's foot. Charillos was declared the winner and Lysander again noted to himself how each boy did seem to have a different strength. He was pleased that Charillos had found something that he was good at.

XII

Helen had got to the stage where she couldn't stand the idea of doing another mathematical problem. Her attention was waning and she was visibly flagging.

"I think it's time for lunch," said Gorga.

Helen suddenly perked up. She was so relieved.

"After lunch," said Gorga. "We will introduce you to the *bibasis* - just to see how good you are and then we will spend the rest of the afternoon learning to sing."

"Learning to sing?" questioned Helen.

"Yes," said Gorga. "We will start with some ridicule singing. I have learnt that young girls your age tend to prefer that kind of singing."

"That sounds fun," said Helen. She remembered what her mother had said and how she could use such a song to embarrass Lysander.

After lunch Gorga was as good as her word. She started by asking Helen to see how high she could jump and then touch her heels to her own buttocks at the top of her jump. Because her mother had told her about this, Helen was not surprised by this request and she knew exactly what to do.

She stood in one place and jumped the highest that she could. At the very top of her jump she flicked her heels backwards and slapped them into her bottom with a light movement. She felt a strong sense of satisfaction as she landed and turned to Gorga for approval.

"Not bad," said Gorga. "Now do it three times in a row."

Helen took a deep breath. She knew from experience that this was going to be tough. She carefully steadied herself and then tried the jump. She managed to fit in the three kicks and touched her buttocks on each one but on the last jump her landing was a little too far forward and she lurched, falling to the floor on her hands and knees. She got up quickly and was angry with herself.

"Don't worry, Helen," said Gorga sympathetically. "It is difficult. I am here to help you. I can see that your legs are strong and you can make the jump. It is now just a question of balance on your landing. I think that you will get it soon. Let's try one more time. Only this time I will hold your hands to help steady you."

Gorga came in front of Helen and held both her hands. "Now, let's try five jumps in a row," said Gorga.

Helen steadied herself again and concentrated hard. She made the jumps and realised that with Gorga's hands to guide her that she tended to land in the same spot as she had taken off from. She didn't get this straight away and she could feel on the first few jumps that

Gorga was pushing her backwards a little to stop her from lunging forwards. It was only a gentle push but Helen could feel it and she realised that she needed to land such that Gorga would not have to push her. She experimented with a few different techniques and, finally, on the fifth jump she tried arching her back and tilting her head slightly back. It seemed to work well.

"Let's do it again," said Helen.

She was keen to see if her new technique would work again. Gorga agreed. So Helen did another five jumps in a row. This time she landed perfectly on each of them.

"Very good," said Gorga. "Now let's try it without me holding you. I will stand in front of you to catch you if you fall but I suspect that I will not need to do that."

Helen nodded her agreement. She knew this was important. If she could master the *bibasis* then she would be able to enter competitions in the main arena in front of everyone and she would become well-known and even famous throughout the whole of Sparta.

Again she took a deep breath and steadied herself. She let go of Gorga's hands and she started to jump. She concentrated hard on her slightly arched back and keeping her head slightly pushed back. In fact Helen concentrated so hard that she ended up losing count of the number of jumps she had done and only stopped when Gorga exclaimed, "that's eight jumps in a row! You can stop now."

Helen stopped. Her face was flushed red with a mixture of pride and energy from the jumping. She couldn't help herself. She rushed forward and put her hands around Gorga. She gave her a big hug and said loudly, "I did it!"

"Yes," said Gorga. "You did really well. I have not seen a young girl master the *bibasis* as quickly as you. I think you are making fine progress with your training. In fact, I will speak to Cleitagora, who runs the state *bibasis* school and see if we can get you enrolled as an apprentice."

Helen nodded in agreement. She knew this was a big thing. The dancers from the state school were the ones who did the dancing at all the major festivals and religious events in Sparta and they were all well-known.

"You will need to continue to practise with me," said Gorga. "You will need to be able to do a hundred jumps in a row to be able to enrol at the state school but I have every confidence you will be able to do that soon. I shall speak to Cleitagora tonight after we have finished. I will also bring some hand bells with me tomorrow so that you can practise with those. All the best *bibasis* dancers hold small bells in both hands and ring them at the same time as they flick their heels onto their buttocks."

XIII

Nikandros was unsure whether to carry on with the training for the afternoon. He had an injured cub and the best thing to do would be to stop and give the cub a chance to heal. But, of course, in battle the enemy did not give wounded soldiers a chance to recover. They would push on regardless. Nikandros thought this through and eventually declared to the boys, "we have four events to complete today. We are due to throw the javelin, we have a boxing competition, a wrestling competition and we will begin to learn the pankration."

Pankration was a kind of mixed martial arts in which the opponents could use boxing and wrestling techniques but also others, such as kicking, holds, joint-locks and chokes on the ground. It was a vicious and difficult sport but it was great training for a warrior.

Nikandros continued to outline his thoughts, "Ariston is injured today and so I have decided to postpone the boxing, the wrestling and the pankration until later to give him a chance to heal and a chance to compete properly. But there is no contact involved in the javelin and so we will complete that competition before we finish for today. Ariston, do you think you can still throw the javelin?"

Ariston nodded sullenly. All the while he

scowled at Leobotas to show him that he considered that Leobotas had dropped the shot put on purpose and that he would aim to get even with him at some stage.

The javelin was a light spear that was designed to fly through the air as far as possible but always landed with the point first so that it stuck into its target. Lysander had played with a javelin before in his garden. His mother had made a model of a soldier out of bags stuffed with cloth and other things and she had given it a small shield with the markings of Athens on it. Lysander had practised throwing the javelin at the Athenian dummy until he had got quite good at it. Lysander thought this might be a good opportunity for him to win something and to show the rest of the boys that he had potential to be a warrior as well. If only his shoulder wasn't hurting from where the discus hit it earlier and his hand didn't still throb from the previous day.

The technique for throwing the javelin involved running a short distance and then whipping the javelin forward using the whole upper body to give it as much momentum as possible. A lot of the force came from the shoulder. So, Lysander was worried that his injuries might hold him back.

Lysander did not need to worry. When the boys saw Nikandros show them how to throw the javelin, they thought it looked easy and were confident that they would do well.

It became obvious, however, that the javelin required good technique as well as strength and none of the boys mastered the technique in any of their three throws. The javelin seemed to go all over the place and it didn't fly very far. Indeed, Pausarius couldn't seem to master the technique at all and his javelins actually travelled through the air sideways so that they didn't even stick into the ground.

Leobotas thought about whether he could pretend that he had got the technique wrong and actually throw the javelin at Lysander. He decided against it in the end because he had already hit him with the discus and injured Ariston with the shot put. He thought that if he were to deliberately mess up the javelin, Nikandros might suspect he was doing it on purpose. Besides, he realised that if he were to hit Lysander with the javelin there was a good chance that he might kill him. Even Leobotas realised that would not be a good thing to do.

Ariston was not able to run up properly but, nonetheless, he still threw the javelin. He actually managed to get it further than the other boys. Lysander smiled as he remembered that he had played the javelin game with Ariston when they were younger. They had both thrown at his Athenian dummy and Ariston must have remembered the skill.

When it came to Lysander's turn he swallowed deeply and tried to block out the pain in his shoulder and hand. He ran up to the line and released the javelin with all the force he could muster. Lysander let out a loud grunt as he did so with the effort of the throw.

It was an impressive effort. The javelin sailed through the air at a perfect forty-five degree angle and span in the air as it flew. Lysander had learned to do this as he knew it made the javelin fly further and straighter. After what seemed a good few seconds in the air the javelin came down and landed perfectly in the ground with the point sticking deep into the earth.

"Excellent," shouted Nikandros. "A throw like that would put the fear of the Gods into the Persians. You are the winner of the javelin for today, Lysander."

Some of the boys came up to Lysander and patted him on the back or congratulated him. All except for Leobotas who just scowled darkly at him.

After this Nikandros told the boys to collect their things and return to camp. Lysander and Leon helped Ariston to walk back as he was still limping a little.

When they got back to the camp Nikandros addressed them again, "I will give you a short while to recover your strength and drink some water. After that we will discuss the subject of leadership again and then I will give you your briefing for tonight. I suspect that you are going to need it."

XIV

Helen and Gorga finished their lunch.

"Right," said Gorga. "You have done well at the *bibasis*. Your legs must still be tired from all that running yesterday and the jumping just now so we will concentrate on singing this afternoon."

"You promised we could learn ridicule singing," reminded Helen.

"Yes," said Gorga. "And that is exactly what we are going to do. Do you know how the ridicule songs work?"

Helen thought about this for a few moments and realised that she had not heard a ridicule song being sung and she didn't really know how to perform one. So, she slowly shook her head.

"The ridicule song," explained Gorga. "Is an important part of the training in the *agoge*."

Helen looked puzzled. What had her singing got to do with Lysander's training in the *agoge*, she wondered.

"You will be invited, along with all the other girls in training to watch the boys training in the *agoge*. If you spot any that you think are not trying hard enough or are not performing well enough then you are encouraged to make up a song about them. You must use the song to humiliate them as much as possible in order to encourage them to train harder. Every month you will be invited to the *agora* and you will be asked to perform your song in front of all the *ephors*. The best song is rewarded with a prize and the boy who is the subject of the song will receive a punishment."

Helen thought about this. She had been looking forward to singing a ridicule song about Lysander but she hadn't realised that he would be punished afterwards if her song was good. She wasn't sure how she felt about this. Deep down she loved her brother. She liked to compete against him and to beat him in sports and competitions and she liked to make fun of him but she didn't want to hurt him or get him hurt.

"The key skill," Gorga went on, "is to make your song rhyme, make it funny and pick on the thing that the subject can't do very well. Your aim is to shame them into trying to do better."

Helen nodded.

"Would you like me to give you an example?" asked Gorga.

"Yes, please," Helen replied.

"I wrote this song on my way here this morning," said Gorga. "Tell me what you think."

Gorga began to sing:

I know a silly girl; her name is Helen.
She can't do sums or numbers.
She can't even run,
she just stumbles and lumbers
she thinks she's pretty,

that she looks like cupid
but we all know, that really,
she's just plain and stupid.

Helen was a bit shocked to hear the song. She thought she had been making progress with Gorga but this song was cruel and made her feel like she had failed again. She replied slowly, "But it's not true. I can run - you said so yourself. I've never claimed to be pretty and I can do mathematics. You saw that this morning."

"It doesn't matter," replied Gorga. "I can tell the song has hurt your pride. As a result, you will try harder next time and that is the point of the song."

Helen thought about this. She understood what Gorga had said but she was still hurt by the song.

"Is that what you really think about me?" she asked.

Gorga smiled at her.

"I am not going to answer that. That is for you to work out."

Gorga paused for a few moments and then she continued. "Now the final thing we are going to do today is to write a ridicule song. I will give you until the morning to compose one. It can be about anyone you like. But if it is not as good as mine I will make you do athletics all day tomorrow and I won't allow you to have any food. That is what they do to the boys in the *agoge* sometimes; so if you want to be as good as the boys maybe you should experience the same conditions as them."

Helen remembered Pylos's words. They used hunger to train the students in the *agoge* - and Gorga had just confirmed that. She felt pleased now that she had sent Pylos on his errand.

After this, Gorga collected her things and left Helen to ponder the task of writing her song.

XV

Lysander was just about to collapse onto his bed as Nikandros had suggested when a small white corner of parchment sticking out in the middle caught his eye. He knew that was not there when they left and so it immediately raised his suspicions.

His natural instinct was to pull it out straight away but he quickly realised that if he did he would be seen by the other boys and that could result in a difficult conversation. Instead, he slowly laid down on his bed and turned sideways so that the piece of parchment was almost covered by his body. By wrapping himself into a curled position he was also able to shield the parchment from all the other boys in case they were watching.

When he was satisfied that he couldn't be seen, he slowly started to pull the parchment out. This had two effects. Firstly, he realised that the parchment was not the only thing in his bed. He realised that someone had carefully hidden and cushioned some eggs and some biscuits in there. Secondly, he immediately recognised Helen's handwriting. He realised straight away that she would not have brought the eggs herself as she would be in her own training programme by now. So, he guessed that she must have asked Pylos to bring them. He knew instantly what a risk Pylos had taken to do this and he was immediately grateful to him. The eggs would make a great addition to their evening feast and he was looking forward to eating them already. However, he did have a problem. He couldn't disclose the fact that they were in his bedding because it would get Helen and Pylos into trouble. He also realised that if he took them out now and pretended to find them in the grass or something, then Leobotas would immediately steal them or, worse, smash them. He had to think of a way to disclose them to the group without getting his family into trouble and without incurring Leobotas's anger.

His thoughts about this were interrupted by Nikandros's voice. Nikandros was speaking to the group. "*Paides*, you have had a chance to rest. Now we must turn to the question of your leader. Leobotas claims to be your leader but he did not have all of your support yesterday. Has he done enough today to change anyone's mind? Do you all now accept him as your leader?"

The boys who had previously supported Leobotas all nodded again and voiced their approval. Nikandros looked at Lysander, Ariston and Leon.

"Well," he said. "What about you three?"

Lysander realised that if he didn't give Leobotas his approval the bullying would continue and maybe get even worse. He thought Leobotas was a terrible leader but nonetheless he found himself slowly nodding his head.

"Yes, I agree," he said. "He is our leader and has my support."

It took a little while for Ariston and Leon to join in, especially Ariston. But after a while even they agreed and nodded their consent.

Nikandros looked at the three of them carefully. He could tell they were not sure. So, after a little while he decided to ask a further question. "The sign of a great leader is someone that not only has the support of his men but also has the love of his men. They would follow him anywhere and gladly die for him. Do you love Leobotas? Do you respect him as your leader? Would you die for him if the need arose?"

It didn't take Lysander very long to think about this. He did not respect Leobotas and he would certainly not die for him. "No, I would not die for him," he said. "He does not have my respect. He believes that force alone is enough to be a leader but he does not understand that leaders have to care for their men and know what they are capable of and not capable of."

Ariston and Leon quickly signalled their agreement with Lysander's words.

"Very well then," said Nikandros. "Leobotas, you will wear the blue cloak for a second day. You have heard the words of your men. Think carefully about what they have said."

If a human face could summon thunder simply by the power of its look then a raging storm would be gathering right now. Leobotas's face was almost black with anger and the look he gave Lysander would have made any other boy tremble on the spot. But Lysander had decided he did not care. He was going to stand up to Leobotas and they were going to elect a different leader.

"I promised at the start of the day," Nikandros continued. "If you are unable to elect a leader that has the support of you all, I will punish you all by making you miss your evening meal again. I know that you have not eaten since breakfast but I must teach you a lesson. You shall continue to miss your meal until you can resolve the issue of your leader."

The boys had known this was coming as soon as Lysander had spoken and they simply looked at the ground in a glum manner.

"There is one thing that might help you this evening," said Nikandros. "In the *agoge* it is permitted for boys to steal food to supplement their rations. If you are caught stealing then you will be punished by the *ephors* but if you can steal without being caught then you are permitted to eat it in your camp."

The boys looked at each other. They knew that Nikandros was not just giving them permission to steal but that he was actually encouraging them to do so. They did not need much encouragement. They had been training all day and they were hungry.

"With that *paides*, I will leave you for tonight. I will return first thing in the morning for your next day of training. Sleep well and I hope you manage to feed your hunger."

Nikandros left the boys for the evening. They all looked at each other, wondering who would speak first.

CHAPTER IV
The raiding party

I

Leobotas was the first to speak. "You heard what Nikandros said. We have permission to steal food so that we can eat tonight. I am hungry and I am fed up with eating one meal a day because of Lysander and Ariston. I will lead a raid to steal food so that we can fill our bellies tonight."

The boys all looked a little uncertain. Eventually, it was Charillos who plucked up the courage to ask. "Where will we steal the food from?"

Leobotas smiled. He had already anticipated this question.

"That's easy," he replied. "We will steal it from the lazy *helots*. There's a farm I know in the *perioikoi* district. It's called Theos Farm. It produces so much food that it often has stalls at the market. It is owned by an elderly couple and they have lots of *helots* working there. We will not steal the old couple's food - they have Sparta's protection - but we will steal the supplies that the *helots* keep for themselves. They are good for nothing and no-one will care if the *helots* go hungry for a day or two. Besides, they are not allowed to stop us or challenge us. So, even if we get caught, the *helots* will not be able to do anything about it. It's a brilliant plan. The kind of plan only a leader would come up with."

Leobotas shot a glance at Lysander as he said his final words. Several of the boys slowly nodded their heads in agreement with Leobotas's suggestion.

Lysander was very uncomfortable with this idea. He thought about how Pylos and Lampita would feel if their food was stolen and he realised the idea was not fair on the *helots*. He decided that this must be the moment that he would stand up to Leobotas. He didn't really have a plan for how to do this but he knew he must say something. He surprised himself as the words tumbled out.

"I don't think that is a good plan, Leobotas," he said. "If we steal the food from the *helots* then they won't be able to work on the farm. That will affect everybody because that farm provides food for many citizens. I think it would be better if we didn't steal but instead we went foraging."

"Foraging? What is that?" asked Charillos.

"Foraging is when you collect food that is growing wild, such as in the forests or at the side of roads," Lysander replied. "On our trip to the Eurotas yesterday I saw lots of olives and figs growing in the groves just away from the roads. I saw a bee's hive so we could collect honey and I noticed a pine forest a little way from the track. We can collect pine nuts and we might find some eggs as well."

He added this last suggestion because he intended to pretend to find the eggs that Pylos had left in his bedding. He realised that he would have to destroy the biscuits because he couldn't pretend to find them at the side of the road.

The boys each thought carefully about what Lysander had proposed. Leobotas was the first to respond. "That sounds like a terrible plan. Collecting food from the side of the road will not give us enough to fill our bellies. Besides, it is the plan of a coward. Nikandros has given us permission to steal and your plan does not involve stealing. Nikandros wants us to prove ourselves. And who can possibly object to stealing from *helots*? You're not a *helot* lover are you?"

Lysander ignored this last question. He knew it was designed to trap him and give Leobotas an excuse to denounce him. Instead, he spoke slowly and clearly.

"Nikandros wants us not to be hungry. He said we could steal if we have to but he didn't say we must steal. He also said we would be punished if we are caught. My plan does not involve the risk of punishment."

There was a little pause while the boys thought over what Leobotas and Lysander had said. It was Ariston who spoke first. "I agree with Lysander," said Ariston. "His plan is much better and I want to go with him."

Leon quickly added, "me too."

Leobotas scowled darkly.

"What about the rest of you?" he asked. "Does anyone else want to go on this coward's mission?"

Charillos surprised himself and was slightly shocked when he heard the words that came out of his own mouth. "I like the idea of foraging and that food sounds nice - honey and eggs are two of my favourite things."

You could tell that Polydoros, Teleklos and Pausarius were a little unsure about what to do. They liked Lysander's idea as well but they had pledged their loyalty to Leobotas. And they were scared of him. Slowly, they all decided that they would support Leobotas rather than Lysander and they agreed to take part in the raid on the farm.

Leobotas wanted the whole group to go together on his raid. He hadn't worked out how yet but he intended to find a way during the raid to ensure that Ariston and Lysander would get caught. They would then be punished by the *ephors* and after that they would not be able to put themselves forward to be leader and so they would have to support him in the role.

Leobotas was about to get up and come towards Lysander and his group. He was thinking about using physical force to get them to change their minds and join in with his plan. But just at the moment that Leobotas was preparing to swing a punch, Lysander spoke up. "Why don't we have two parties on two different raids tonight? We can see which party collects the most food and Leobotas, if you win, Ariston, Leon and I will agree to give you our support as our leader. How does that sound?"

Leobotas thought about it for a moment. He was certain that he could steal more food from the *helots* than Lysander and his group could forage and this might be a way to settle the dispute about his leadership once and for all. He hated wearing the blue cloak and was desperate to be able to take it off and wear a red cloak like everyone else.

"I agree," he sneered. "You don't stand a chance."

As a result, the boys started to split into two groups. One contained Lysander, Ariston, Leon and Charillos and they started to discuss their plan for where to go, what they would need to take to forage with and what time to set off.

"We should go now," said Lysander, "while it is still light so that we can see what we are collecting."

The boys agreed and were just about to leave the camp when Lysander had a final thought. "Wait, we will each need a bag to collect our food in," Lysander said. "Can anyone think where we can get some quickly?

It took only a few moments before Leon spoke up. "Our *helots* always bring our food in bags. Perhaps we could steal those."

"We are not stealing from *helots*," replied Lysander calmly. "We will ask them if we can borrow them. People treat you better if you ask them things rather than tell them. Charillos - you are good with words. Do you think you can find our *helots* and ask them if we could borrow their bags please?"

Lysander didn't really think that Charillos was good with words. This was the first time that Charillos had joined them and so Lysander wanted Charillos to feel that he was a part of their group. He wanted to give him something easy to do, so that he would be pleased with himself.

"Of course," said Charillos, who was indeed both proud to have been asked and pleased to have a task.

He disappeared quickly and returned shortly afterwards holding four cloth bags.

"They were happy to help," he said. "They just want the bags back in the morning so that they don't get into trouble with Nikandros. I promised them that we would return them as soon as we have finished with them."

Lysander smiled broadly and thanked Charillos. With that the party set off. Even though they were hungry and tired after the day's training and they carried a few bruises from Leobotas's treatment, there was an energy and a purpose in their strides and they moved over the ground quickly.

The group that remained - Leobotas, Teleklos, Polydoros and Pausarius - also gathered together to make their plan. "We should wait until dark," said Leobotas. "In that way, we can get into the farm and steal as much as we can without being seen. The lazy *helots* will all be asleep."

II

While all this was happening, Helen was at home reflecting on her day. She was sitting down to a lovely meal prepared for her by Pylos and Lampita. She wondered what Lysander would be doing now and if he had got the eggs. She hoped that he would be grateful. She imagined him thanking her when they next got to meet - although she wasn't sure when that was going to be. She also thought about Gorga and what had happened since her training had begun. She was very confused about the whole thing. Firstly, she had started off really disliking Gorga and felt that she had been way too mean to her. Then she reflected how Gorga seemed to have mellowed a little and had even praised her a bit. But the ridicule song that Gorga had sung confused her again. It seemed that Gorga didn't like her after all and that she considered her just a silly little girl - which Helen was sure that she was not. And now, she had to write a ridicule song that she must sing to Gorga tomorrow. Helen had no idea what to sing about or how to go about writing it. She thought and thought about it but she was just stuck - she couldn't think what to say. It bothered her that she was stuck and it showed on her face. She was mostly scowling and unhappy throughout the whole of the evening meal. Eventually, her mother, Demetria, put down her fork and turned to Helen.

"What's the matter, Helen?" she asked. "You've been quiet and grumpy throughout the whole meal tonight. It's not like you at all."

Helen decided to confide in her mother. "Well, Mother," she said, "I am not sure whether Gorga likes me or not and I have to write a practice ridicule song by tomorrow morning and I have no idea where to start or who to sing it about."

"Don't worry about Gorga," Demetria said. "She's always like that. It's her way. She always treated me as though she hated me and she would say the most cruel things. But she doesn't really mean them. It's just her way of toughening you up and it must work because she is one of the most sought after trainers in the whole of Sparta."

Helen nodded. She recognised that what her mother was saying was true and that she would just have to get used to being told off by Gorga.

"Why don't you write your ridicule song about Gorga?" suggested her mother. "You need to think of the one thing that is her biggest weakness. The thing that will hurt her the most and focus on that."

Helen thought about this for a moment. She liked the idea of getting her own back on Gorga but she wasn't sure that Gorga had any obvious weaknesses.

"But I don't know what to write about her," said Helen. "I don't know her that well and she doesn't seem to have any weaknesses as far as I can see."

Her mother smiled. "She is old," she said. "Like all old people she hates getting old and wishes she could be young again. Why don't you focus on the fact that she is old," her mother said with another smile and a wink.

Helen decided that was good advice and that she would go to her room to work on the ridicule song. She got into bed to compose it so that she could fall asleep straight away and wake up fresh and alert in the morning.

///

Lysander took his little group away from the camp so that they couldn't be overheard by Leobotas and his group. "We will need to work fast," he said. "It will be dark in a couple of hours."

The boys all nodded very seriously. Each one of them realised that something very important had happened. Lysander had rebelled against Leobotas and they had supported Lysander. They would be traitors in Leobotas's eyes and so it was crucial that they win the competition to collect the most food.

Lysander spoke to them again. "I think we should follow the same route that we took yesterday to get to the Eurotas. I saw lots of olives and figs growing at the side of the path. I also remember there was a beehive that we can collect some honey from and I am sure I could smell a pine forest up on the ridge. We should be able to collect lots of food if we follow that route."

The boys nodded in agreement. They knew the way to the Eurotas and it didn't take long before they picked up the same path that they had taken the previous day. They quickly started to notice wild olive trees growing at the side of the road and various bushes with berries of different kinds. Their bags started to fill with the fruits of the forest and the path. It was not long before they reached the place where Lysander had found the salix tree and even though it was beginning to get a little dark now, Lysander was able to find it again. He was relieved to see that the beehive was still there. He smiled to himself as he caught the faint whiff of pine resin. He had been right. There was a pine forest close by. There would be lots of pine nuts. He knew that pine nuts were both tasty and filling because

Lampita had fed them to him when he was younger as she made pine nut cakes. Lysander was relieved. This was great news.

"Ariston, Leon," he said. "I will collect the honey from this hive with Charillos. Can you please find the pine forest that I can smell and begin to collect pine nuts? Charillos and I will come to find you once we have the honey."

"Of course," both boys said. They quickly scampered off up the hill.

Lysander and Charillos looked at the beehive.

"How are we going to get to it?" asked Charillos. "It's quite high up."

"If I stand on your shoulders, I think I can reach it," said Lysander. "Do you think you can take my weight, Charillos?"

"I am sure I can," he replied quickly.

And so, using the trunk of the tree to steady himself, Lysander managed to climb up onto Charillos's shoulders and using his *xyele* he was able to reach the hive at his fullest stretch. He decided to take only half of the hive as that would leave the bees with something to eat and the colony could continue to live. The colony would repair and build itself a new hive quickly, provided it had some food to live on.

So, Lysander cut a big chunk off the hive with his *xyele* and climbed down from Charillos's shoulders. He then wrapped the honeycomb in tree leaves so that the honey did not make his bag too sticky and then placed it carefully inside.

After that it was not long before he and Charillos found the other boys and helped them to collect a bumper crop of pine nuts.

It was beginning to get dark and so they decided to return to the camp. Each of their bags was bulging with food and they were very pleased with themselves. Lysander quickly made his way to his own bedding and, in the fading light he quickly added to his own bag, the eggs that Pylos had supplied him with earlier. He crumbled the biscuits into small pieces and scattered them in the dust.

Leobotas and his team were nowhere to be seen.

"Let's wait until Leobotas and his team get back before we eat any food," Lysander said. "We need to be able to compare what we have both gathered so that we can see who is the winner. I suggest that we get a little sleep until then."

The boys flopped down onto their bedding and started to get some well-earned rest.

IV

Just as the light had begun to fade, only shortly before Lysander and his group returned, Leobotas had turned to his group. "Right, let's get going. Let's make sure we steal as much food as we can. I want to see the look on Lysander's face when we beat him!"

Leobotas's group laughed loudly among

themselves. They were looking forward to having full bellies tonight, to bullying a few *helots* and, most of all, to seeing the disappointment on Lysander's face.

They all felt sure that this was the moment that Leobotas would be confirmed as their leader and his cloak would change from blue to red. Polydoros, Teleklos and Pausarius each felt sure that they would benefit from having supported Leobotas all along. They hoped they would get bigger rations and less work duty to do as a result.

The boys moved off quickly in single file in the direction of the farm. It was about half an hour away and so when they arrived it was well and truly dark. The night sky provided them with a near perfect blanket of invisibility. There was a half moon that provided a little light but not so much that they could easily be seen.

As they arrived at the boundary of the farm they stopped to survey the scene. They could see very little, as it was quite dark and much of the farm was in shadow. On one side there were a series of animal holding pens and they could tell these were occupied because occasional animal noises came from that direction. There was a collection of buildings on the other side. Some of these buildings had windows and some had faint candlelight coming from inside. These were the ones that were occupied and the boys knew they had to avoid them.

Leobotas gathered his cubs closer to him and spoke in a low voice. "Right, we need to know where the food stores are kept. So, we are going to have to split up and search the buildings inside to see what is stored there. Don't approach the buildings that have a light in them because that means there are people inside. Pausarius - go check out the animals. If there is a small one like a piglet or a lamb then we can take it with us. Let's all do a reconnaissance and meet back here to report."

The boys nodded. Their faces looked serious as their earlier excitement had now changed to anxiety and a little fear when they were presented with the reality of what they were about to do. Leobotas had one last thing to say. "Remember what Nikandros said," he reminded them. "We are allowed to steal but not to get caught. If you get caught by *helots* feel free to kick and punch them as hard as you can. If you get caught by Spartans or *perioikoi* then don't say anything about the other members of the group. Keep quiet and take the punishment yourself. When I whistle, come back here and we will compare notes."

The boys then split up and headed off in various directions to see what they could find. Pausarius quickly made it to the animal pens and skirted all the way round the outside of them on his hands and knees. He could see a lot of goats, a few pigs and a couple of horses. Some of the pigs were young ones and he was sure he could carry away one of the smaller piglets.

Polydoros had less luck. The building he decided to search was very dark inside and it took a little while for his eyes to adjust. He gained the impression that this was a large shed where the farming tools were kept. As he searched around in the dark he bumped into a rake and knocked it over. It fell to the floor with a clatter. Polydoros froze to the spot hoping that no-one had heard the noise but after a few moments he began to hear voices and people whispering together in a concerned way. He decided that it would be better if he left now rather than be caught red-handed. So, he made for the door and quickly ran back to the meeting spot before he could be spotted.

Pausarius was just thinking about whether he should steal the piglet now or whether he should report back first. His choice was made easy. It was just at the point when he had decided that he would step into the pen and grab the piglet that he heard the sound of the rake falling and then the sound of people's voices. He quickly changed his mind and moved back to the agreed spot.

Teleklos was similarly unlucky. The building he chose was full of food for the animals. There was lots of grain and scraps of old and rotting fruit and vegetables. The kind of thing that a human could eat but, only if they were desperate, as it would not make a tasty feast. It was just as he was deciding to search another building that he heard the noise of the rake falling to the ground from a nearby building and then the sound of voices and lanterns getting close. Like Polydoros and Pausarius he decided that it would be better to return now rather than wait to be caught.

Leobotas, on the other hand, had much better luck. He found a building that was heaving with food. It had many pieces of meat hanging from the rafters to dry and cure. There were barrels of many different kinds of food and it was easy to get the lid off these. There were olives, there were stuffed vine leaves, there were nuts, there were vegetables of every size and variety and shelves groaning with the weight of the fruit upon them. Leobotas's heart jumped for joy. There was everything here that they would need. He just had to get the other boys to come and help him and they would have a massive feast tonight. He was just making his way back to the meeting point when he heard the noise of the rake and the sound of people coming to investigate. He moved quickly to the agreed spot and waited for the others to return. It didn't take long.

"What happened?" demanded Leobotas.

Polydoros had no choice but to own up.

"It was me," he admitted. "I stumbled into a rake in the dark. It fell over and the noise has attracted people to come and look. We are never going to get anything now." He started to whimper a little.

"Shussh," ordered Leobotas. "We are all here, so they are not going to discover anything. They will go back to the house soon and then we will have our chance. I have discovered the barn with all the food. There is more than we can carry. So, we just have to be patient."

"And I have found a piglet that we can steal," whispered Pausarius. "We can drink its blood mixed with oats and then we can make bacon."

The other boys looked at Pausarius with a quizzical look. They liked the idea of bacon but not more of the pigs blood porridge - they would get that for breakfast in the morning anyway and it was not exactly tasty.

Leobotas decided not to respond. He simply turned back to the matter in hand.

"Right, let's lie low, let's be quiet and let's give it some time before we move back in."

V

Helen was getting tired. She had laid on her bed for ages trying to think of a song but it was getting late and she was beginning to get sleepy. She forced herself to think about it one more time.

What had her mother said? "*No-one likes getting old.*"

That was obviously one thing that Helen could focus on. She started to form a little couplet in her head.

"Gorga is old

and her heart is cold."

That could work, she thought. "*I will have to remember that,*" she said to herself.

Then another thought occurred to her of how well respected Gorga was and how much Gorga thought of herself as being an important person in Sparta because she was in demand to train all the young girls who were at the age when their training needed to start. Helen thought that something which talked about Gorga's pride and how to puncture it would also be good. She started to compose some more lines in her head.

"Gorga thinks she's brilliant

but really she's just incoherent...."

No, Helen thought to herself. *That's not good enough. I will have to try harder.*

Shortly after that, Helen slipped into an uneasy sleep. Her body needed her not to be awake but her mind kept coming back to the words of the ridicule song.

She was stuck in this unfortunate dance for most of the night - slipping between deep sleep and restlessness while thinking about her song. It was going to be a long night.

VI

"We have waited for about half an hour," whispered Leobotas. "All has gone quiet. Even some of the lights have been put out. This is our chance. Teleklos, Polydoros and I will raid the main barn. We will steal as much food as we can carry. Pausarius, I want you to give us a little while to get to the barn and start collecting food. Then I want you to go to the animal pens and steal that piglet. If we bring home some bacon then even Lysander will have to admit defeat and accept that I am a better leader."

The boys all nodded their agreement.

Eventually, Teleklos spoke up with a question. "What shall we carry the food in, Leobotas? We have no bags."

Leobotas paused for a moment and a frown crossed his face. It was clear that he hadn't thought about this. Then he had what he considered to be a brilliant idea. "We'll use my blue cloak," he said. "If you and Polydoros hold it in each corner you can carry a lot of food between you. I will see if I can find a bag or a sack or something to carry more food in. Pausarius, when you have captured the piglet you can wrap it in your cloak to stop it squealing. That should work. Is that all clear?"

Once again, the boys nodded their heads in agreement.

"Let's go," said Leobotas.

The boys all got up from their hiding position and moved quickly towards the barn which they knew contained enough food to fill their bellies for a month. Pausarius was supposed to wait a while before starting out for the piglet but he was so nervous and excited that he forgot and ran pretty much straight away as soon as Leoboatas and the others had left.

Leobotas felt that his plan was going well. He and the other boys reached the barn quickly and they slipped inside easily. Unfortunately, all the lights had now been extinguished and it was very dark inside the barn. A small sliver of moonlight entered through an upper storey skylight and that provided the only illumination.

"Don't move," whispered Leobotas to the other boys. "We will have to wait a little while for our eyes to get adjusted to the light. Don't move so that we don't bang into anything and make a noise."

And so the boys stood stock still trying to squint into the darkness to see what they could. Slowly shapes started to emerge out of the darkness. They began to make out the shape of barrels and sacks and jars of things spread throughout the barn.

"Take my cloak," said Leobotas. "Start to fill it with whatever food you can find in those barrels and sacks. I will carry as many of those jars that I can."

The boys started to clumsily fill the cloak with as much food as they could. They couldn't really see what it was but Teleklos put his hand into one barrel and instantly realised it was olives preserved in oil as his hand got sticky and wet very quickly. He was a big fan of olives and so put a few large scoops of olives into the cloak. Along with all the oil, this made the cloak wet and sticky very quickly.

It was just at this point that the boys heard a loud series of squeals coming from outside. Pausarius had found his piglet but he had never caught one before and so didn't really appreciate how fast and agile they could be. He had slipped into the pen easily enough and the moon outside meant that he spotted the piglet quickly. He moved towards it and tried to grab it with both hands and wrap it in his cloak. The piglet had other ideas and easily evaded his snatches. It ran around its pen squealing at the top of its voice alerting its mother so that she could help. Unfortunately, its mother was in the next pen and so all she could do was come to the fence and squeal loudly as well, so as to frighten off the intruder. The effect of two pigs squealing at the top of their voices was truly loud. Pausarius quickly stopped what he was doing and tried to calm the pigs down by "shushing" them loudly. This had no effect whatsoever and it did not take long before the owners of the farm and all its *helots* were awake. They started to light their candles, get dressed and come out of their houses to discover what was happening.

Pausarius was the first to take action. He realised that he was not going to capture the piglet before someone caught him and so he shouted to the other boys, "Run, we're going to get caught!"

After that he leaped over the pens and ran back to their hiding place as quickly as he could. The other boys heard him in the barn and started to panic. Leobotas told them to hold steady but, of course, the sound of Pausarius's voice made the owners realise that it was humans that were in their farm. They had thought it might be foxes, or worse, wolves but Pausarius's shout told them it was people. Leobotas heard someone shout.

"Quick make for the barn. They are stealing our food. Bring some weapons. They may be armed."

At this point, even Leobotas realised the game was up. He whispered hastily to the other boys. "Quick, let's get out before we get caught. Carry as much as you can but move quickly."

Teleklos and Polydoros gathered the corners of the cloak together and started to run as best they could. Leobotas was about to leave empty handed but just as he turned to flee he bumped into a string of sausages and hams that were hanging from the ceiling to dry and cure.

At first he didn't know what they were but he quickly recognised the smell of sausages and grabbed a string, putting it around his neck. He also grabbed two hams - one in each hand - and ran as quick as he could.

So, at this point the boys were in three groups. Pausarius had a head start and was already the furthest from the farm. Leobotas was next. Although he was carrying sausages and hams he could run freely and because he was a big strong boy he made quick progress. Teleklos and Polydoros were dropping further and further behind. They had discovered that it was not easy to run when holding a cloak full of heavy food. It was clear that some of the faster members of the farm were catching them up and Polydoros noticed that at least one of the chasers was carrying a sword. This person didn't look like a *helot* and he realised this person would be within the law to kill them both on the spot as they had just robbed the farm. Polydoros's courage left him. He dropped his corner of the blue cloak and shouted to Teleklos, "Run for your life! They are going to kill us!"

As soon as Polydoros dropped his corner of the cloak all the food inside came tumbling out and spilled on the floor. Teleklos held on tightly to his corner but it was no use - all the food had gone. Teleklos pulled the cloak close to him and then ran as fast as his legs could carry him.

VII

The boys ran for as long and as hard as they could. They were each panting and exhausted. Their lungs felt like bursting until each of them could run no longer. They had got far away from the farm and the chasers had given up a long way back but they had become separated from each other. Without realising it they had all run back in the direction of their *agoge* camp and they were not too far from home. Leobotas stood still for a little while. His chest heaving and panting as he tried to get his breath back. Eventually he felt that he had enough breath to issue a call, "Teleklos, Polydoros, Pausarius, are any of you there?" he shouted into the darkness.

It took a little while but after a few moments he heard a breathless reply.

"Leobotas, is that you?" It was unmistakably the voice of Teleklos. "I have Polydoros with me but he can't speak yet."

Leobotas moved towards the sound of the voice and was hugely relieved to see Teleklos and Polydoros sitting down, each slowly getting their breath back.

Once he had reunited with them he asked them a quick question. "Did you manage to get any food?"

They both shook their heads.

"I did manage to keep your cloak though," Teleklos said helpfully.

At first, Leobotas was angry.

"What did you keep that for?" he demanded. "I hate that cloak."

"If I had left it at the farm then it would have given them a clue that we were there," replied Teleklos. "You are the only person in the whole of Sparta right now who is wearing a blue cloak."

"Oh, you're right," said Leobotas. "Thank you."

"What have you got around your neck?" asked Polydoros. "And what's that in your hands?"

Leobotas let out a broad smile.

"It's two hams and a string of sausages," he smiled. "We didn't leave empty handed. We are going to have a feast tonight and I am not going to give any to Lysander or his stupid friends. We have earned this ourselves. To the victor, the spoils."

Teleklos and Polydoros let out a huge smile and they both started laughing with pleasure. Leobotas joined in for a few moments. He only stopped when he remembered Pausarius was still missing.

"Pausarius, are you there?" he shouted loudly into the night.

In reply, he heard a little whimper that sounded like, "*Help*!"

Leobotas got up quickly and started to

make his way towards the noise. Teleklos and Polydoros followed behind as they were still a little out of breath. In the darkness it was difficult to see where they were going and they had to tread carefully. Just as Leobotas was getting close to where he thought the voice had come from, a figure suddenly jumped out into the path and stood in front of him.

"Hand that meat over," the voice said.

"Who's that?" demanded Leobotas.

"I am not yet worthy of a name. I am a *kruptoi* and I am hungry. Think yourself lucky that you are not a *helot*. I would kill you on the spot. I can see that you are *paides* for you carry the blue cloak of shame. That means you do not have a leader and you are bad *paides*. Now give me the meat before I take out my *xyele* and gut you like the useless boys that you are."

Leobotas had come too far and gone through too much to give up his food as easily as that. He looked the *kruptoi* up and down and decided that he was not that much taller than him. He calculated that with three *paides* against one *kruptoi* they stood a chance of keeping their food.

As these thoughts were going through Leobotas's mind, the *kruptoi* teenager swiftly stepped forward and brought his knee violently into Leobotas's stomach. Leobotas doubled up in pain. As his head went down, the *kruptoi* grabbed his head by the hair, lifted it up so that it was level with his face and then gave Leobotas the hardest punch he had ever experienced straight in his face.

Leobotas instantly collapsed onto the ground half- unconscious. Teleklos and Polydoros both watched with horror as the *kruptoi* took the sausages from around Leobotas's neck and snatched the hams from the floor where Leobotas had dropped them.

"Do either of you two want to challenge me for this food?" the *kruptoi* snarled.

Teleklos and Polydoros both quickly shook their heads.

"Good," he said. "Your other friend is back there, by the way."

And with that, the *kruptoi* turned on his heels and slipped off into the darkness. He disappeared just as quickly as he had appeared.

VIII

Leobotas and the other boys made a sorry sight as they returned to the camp. Leobotas had blood streaming from his face from a deep cut on his cheek. Pausarius also had cuts and bruises to his face. His wrists were cut from where he had been tied up by the *kruptoi*.

The noise they made as they came back quickly roused Lysander and his small party from their sleep.

"What happened? Are you alright?" asked Ariston.

"We found lots of food," said Teleklos. "But we nearly got caught trying to steal it."

"Did anyone see you?" asked Charillos.

"No, we got away without being caught," said Pausarius. "But then we got jumped on by a *kruptoi*. He stole all our food, he beat up Leobotas and tied me to a tree."

Leobotas scowled. He did not say a word. The shame of returning empty handed burned on his face.

"Poor you," said Leon. "You all look like you have had a bad time of things."

"Yes," said Lysander. "You must also be hungry. We have been waiting for you until we ate what we gathered. There's plenty for everyone. Look, I even managed to find a few eggs. We can make a fantastic omelette with these and there's lots of honey and nuts for afterwards."

Even his own team did not know about the eggs and they all showed their delight as Lysander shared this bit of good news.

Teleklos, Polydoros and Pausarius all enthusiastically nodded their approval and gratitude.

Spartans did not often cook. They left that to the *helots*. But when they were on campaign with the army they did sometimes cook for themselves. This felt like one of those moments when they should not wake the *helots* and they should cook for themselves. As a result, the boys set about cooking the food and serving it into portions for everyone.

Without saying a word, Leobotas removed himself from the group and went to sit on his own away from the rest of them and the food that was being prepared.

He was starving hungry, his face hurt and he wanted nothing more than to tuck into a hearty meal. But he didn't want to admit defeat. He couldn't bring himself to accept that Lysander had beaten him and that Lysander would now become leader.

Leobotas decided that he would still oppose Lysander's election so that Lysander would have the shame of having to wear the blue cloak like he had done. He decided to himself that, although he knew the other boys would all support Lysander as their leader tomorrow, he would never agree. He would make Lysander wear the blue cloak forever.

When the food was ready all the boys tucked into it with gusto. They were all starving and although each of them had had their going away feast only a few nights ago, this meal tasted like the best one they had ever had. Each of them was grateful to Lysander and they all knew that when Nikandros came in the morning they would vote for him.

Lysander was still worried though. He had clearly won the challenge but he could see that Leobotas was still in a bad mood and he was worried about what Leobotas would do. Lysander realised that if he was to be the leader of this group he must have the support of all the boys - even Leobotas. His father's words came back to him again. He must have the support of the whole group and, even though he had bullied him, that meant Leobotas as well.

He picked up the plate with the food for Leobotas that was sitting uneaten on the ground. He added a few more olives and figs to it. Leon saw this and guessed Lysander's intentions.

"Shall I call him over?" Leon asked.

"No," replied Lysander. "I will speak with him myself."

He took the plate and wandered over to where Leobotas was sitting. Leobotas refused to look him in the eye and simply stared at the ground.

"You know, you are brave and strong, Leobotas," Lysander said. "You will make a fine Spartan warrior and I have no doubt that you will kill many Athenians and even more Persians. Any army would be proud to have a soldier like you in its ranks."

Leobotas was taken by surprise. He hadn't expected to hear Lysander praise him. He had expected Lysander to taunt him because he had beaten him in the food challenge. That is what he would have done to Lysander if he had won the contest.

"What do you want?" he said slowly. "Why

don't you leave me in peace?"

"I want you to join me, Leobotas," Lysander said. "I want you to eat, to regather your strength and I want you and I to work together."

"How do you want to do that?" asked Leobotas, feeling a little confused.

Lysander paused for a moment and then decided that his moment was now or never. He started to lay out his plan.

"When Nikandros comes tomorrow, he will ask who is to be the leader of our pack. By the terms of our agreement, I have the right to be the leader. But, I will say that I want to be leader only on the condition that you are my second-in-command. Teleklos, Polydoros and Pausarius clearly respect you and they will follow you. I want you to be by my side so that we can work together to make this pack the best of *paides* in the whole of this year's *agoge*. What do you say? Will you help me to lead?"

Leobotas was taken aback. Although it was only a few moments ago that he had decided never to support Lysander, he was touched by Lysander's generosity and flattered by this offer. If he was the second-in-command then it would still bring honour to his family and he could hold his head high. Against his better instincts, he heard himself saying the following words, "I could do that. Especially if you give me that food. I am faint with hunger."

Lysander gave him a huge smile, handed him

the plate of food and slapped him on the back.

"That's great news," said Lysander. "We are going to make a great team. Why don't you come over to the fire when you are ready and tell the other boys. They will be pleased to hear it."

Leobotas stood up and came over with Lysander. He looked a little sheepish, but for the first time, he had half a smile on his lips.

"Well done Charillos, Ariston, Leon and Lysander. You have gathered a great feast. You have helped Lysander to win his bet and he will be our leader in the morning. We have spoken and I am going to help him. Does anyone have a problem with that?"

The boys all broke out into smiles and congratulations. They were all so relieved to hear this news and they all said so very loudly indeed. The camp was a happy sight to behold.

"There's just one more thing we must do," said Lysander. "We must destroy the blue cloak that Teleklos has brought back. That blue cloak is a sign of shame for this pack that we must put behind us. But, more importantly, that cloak could tie you boys to the raid on the farm. It is covered in olive oil and bits of food that could only come from a food store. So, we must destroy it before Nikandros sees it in the morning."

The boys all nodded. They realised that Lysander was right and even more they realised that they were making the right choice in having him as their leader.

"May I?" asked Leobotas as he picked up the cloak and held it over the fire.

"Be my guest, second-in-command," replied Lysander.

And with that, Leobotas dropped the hated blue cloak into the fire. The fact that it was covered in oil made it burn brightly and the boys watched with wide eyes as the flames shot high into the Spartan night.

It was not long after that that they slowly fell asleep with full bellies and were feeling happy for the first time since they had arrived in the *agoge*.

IX

Helen woke up early. She had slept only fitfully but she awoke with a sense of purpose. With a germ of an idea for her ridicule song she quickly got dressed and ran to the writing table so that she could write it down.

As soon as she had finished, she stood back to admire it. Helen sang it to herself in her head and made a couple of small changes. She was finally satisfied. She believed her song was hurtful because it picked up on Gorga's sense of pride and her age. She couldn't wait to try it out on Gorga.

She didn't have long to wait. She had a quick breakfast and no sooner had she finished than Pylos came into the kitchen.

"Mistress Gorga is at the door, Mistress Helen," he announced.

Helen paused. She would normally just acknowledge Pylos with a nod of her head. But this morning she gave him a longer look than she would normally do. She breathed deeply and decided to do something that no Spartan would normally do. She spoke to Pylos as an equal.

"How did it go the other morning, Pylos? Did you manage to deliver the eggs to Lysander?"

"Yes, Mistress," replied Pylos. "I found Lysander's camp. He wasn't there but I found out which was his bed and I left the eggs and your note tucked deeply in the bedding where only he could find them."

"How did you get inside?" asked Helen.

She was confused that it had been so easy for Pylos to find Lysander's bed. She had imagined that the boys were training in a military academy. She had never been to Mentos Field but she imagined a big building there just like the main barracks in central Sparta with guards on the door.

"It's not a building, Mistress," Pylos explained. "They are staying in a field - Mentos Field."

Helen was confused by this answer but at that moment she didn't have time to question Pylos further. Gorga was waiting and she must attend her for the day's training.

Gorga greeted Helen with a wry smile.

"So," she said, "have you prepared your ridicule song? I hope it is good. I don't want any of your nonsense this morning."

"Yes, I am ready," replied Helen.

"Good," said Gorga. "Let's hear it then."

"It's about you," said Helen. "It goes as follows:

Gorga dreams of her talents being told;
she thinks her training is made of gold;
but all she does is scowl and scold.
Really she's just old and her heart is cold;
her hair is bad and her clothes smell of mould.
Gorga's end will soon be foretold.

Gorga listened to the song in silence. Her face didn't betray any emotion. It was impossible to tell whether she liked it or not. Helen felt sure it had done the trick but Gorga gave her no clue at all as to whether she thought it was good or not.

Gorga stared at Helen for a good long while. Eventually, she broke the silence by announcing in a very curt voice. "Right, we will practise boxing this morning."

"But, I thought we were going to start athletics this morning?" said Helen. "Besides, I don't think women do boxing, do they?"

"They do today," replied Gorga.

She then shouted out to attract Pylos's attention, "*Helot* boy, bring us some bandages and a bowl of water."

Pylos did as he was asked.

"Right," said Gorga to Helen. "Hold out your hands while I bind them."

And with that Gorga started the process of wrapping bandages tightly around Helen's hands. Once she had done a complete layer of bandages she then made the bandages wet with the water and then applied another layer. There were four layers in total and Helen could feel that her hands were solid and thick. She could hardly move her fingers but she felt that she could punch a wall and not get hurt.

"Are you going to wear bandages?" Helen asked.

"No," replied Gorga. "The bandages are to protect the boxer's hands from getting damaged. I am not going to hit you so I don't need protection."

Helen was confused by this answer. She had always thought that the purpose of the bandages was to protect the opponent's face, not the boxer's hands. Gorga didn't give her any time to dwell on this though. She continued with her instructions.

"Right, stand in front of me. Put your right foot forward and your right hand out in front. When you try to punch me, move your legs according to which hand you punch with. Do you understand? Are you ready?"

Helen nodded and she took a swing at Gorga. She didn't give it her full force as she didn't want to hit Gorga too hard. Gorga just took a step back and easily avoided the punch. She looked at Helen and simply raised an eyebrow so as to say, "*Was that your best effort?*"

Helen swung again. This time a little harder but still not with her full force. This time Gorga didn't move. She simply swayed her body in the opposite direction to Helen's punch and as she moved she clapped Helen about the ears. She used an open hand rather than a fist but she still hit with some force.

The impact knocked Helen off balance and because the slap had landed on her ears it made a really loud noise in her head, which she shook quickly to try and recover, feeling the noise ringing in her ears.

Helen treated Gorga with a bit more respect now. She didn't swing wildly at her. Instead she started to move around her in a kind of dancing motion and kept jabbing at her so as to see if she could find any weakness in Gorga's defence.

She kept this up for a little while until she could feel her arms and legs getting tired. In frustration she decided to have another attack. Helen danced a little more and then launched a full frontal attack on Gorga. She lunged forwards and tried to hit her with a big blow into her belly.

Gorga saw it coming again and simply stepped out of the way. As the momentum of Helen's punch carried her forwards and past Gorga, Gorga slapped her on the other ear.

Helen stopped and put down her hands. "This is not fun," she said, "I can't hit you and my ears are burning. Why do you keep hitting my ears?"

"Do you not want me to hit your ears?" asked Gorga.

"No, I don't," said Helen as she shook her head.

"Let's take a break and we will try again afterwards," said Gorga. "I promise not to hit your ears any more. Don't take your strapping off."

So, Helen and Gorga sat down together to drink a glass of milk that Pylos brought them both.

"You may be able to write a ridicule song," Gorga said. "But you're not very good at boxing. You have to fool your opponent. You have to catch them off guard and then hit them when they are unbalanced or distracted. Do you understand?"

Helen nodded. She thought she knew what to do and was ready to give it a try.

So, the sparring started again. Helen danced around Gorga a lot, she tried faints and jabs before launching actual punches. But in every case Gorga simply moved out of the way or swayed to one side to avoid the hit. It was very frustrating and Helen was getting very tired and quite mad.

Eventually, Gorga pointed to a spot just

above Helen's head and with a concerned look on her face she announced, "watch out, there's a wasp just above your head!"

Helen stopped instantly. She let down her guard and looked up very briefly to see the wasp. But there was no wasp to be seen. At the very moment that her gaze was coming back down to focus on Gorga again; Gorga took a step forwards and punched her quite hard on the nose. The force of the blow knocked Helen backwards and she instinctively put her hands to her nose because of the pain. After she had touched her face, she was very dismayed to see that the bandages around her hands were now covered in blood as her nose was bleeding profusely.

"See," said Gorga. "You were distracted and I landed a punch. I would have boxed your ears but you told me not to. So, I only did as you asked!"

Helen didn't know what to say. She was burning with rage. Gorga was clearly taunting her and she felt like she might have broken her nose.

"Let's leave it there for the morning," said Gorga, "I think you've learned your lesson."

X

Nikandros returned as usual the next morning. He usually came at first light but this morning he was a little later. This gave the boys time to sweep the camp, clean themselves and tidy up after their feast last night. One or two of them had some cuts and bruises from their adventures but once they had tidied and cleaned up, they and the camp looked much better.

"How did you get on last night, *paides*?" asked Nikandros. "Did you get full bellies?"

The boys were a little unsure of how to reply. They didn't want to say or do anything that would get them in trouble and they knew there was a chance of that. Nikandros pressed them for an answer.

"Do you remember what I told you? It's permitted to steal so long as you don't get caught." He paused for effect, looking carefully at the faces of each of the boys for a clue that would give them away. Each of the boys felt uncomfortable. As his eyes bored into them each began to feel the pressure of his gaze. For some their hair stood on end, others began to sweat a little or experience a knot tightening in their stomachs. Some felt all three.

Nikandros eventually broke the silence. "The *ephors* have received a report this morning that a pack of boys, most likely *paides*, were seen trying to steal from Theos Farm last night. The thieves tried to carry away the food in a cloak but they dropped it and managed to escape. Do you boys know anything about this?"

Lysander decided it was time that he demonstrated his newly agreed leadership skills to the other boys. He stepped forward and said in a firm voice, "It is a serious matter to try to steal from Theos Farm. That farm provides a lot of food for Sparta. But I can assure you, Nikandros, we went nowhere near that farm last night. We collected our food from the hills and open ground that surrounds Sparta. We lived off the land - just like an army would do on the march. We can show you what remains of the food we collected if that would help."

Nikandros smiled to himself. He thought this was a good answer and he was pleased with Lysander. However, he didn't want to let the boys off the hook just yet.

"Very well," he said. "Let me see your cloaks then. The thieves tried to steal the food in their cloaks. If you are telling me the truth, your cloaks should be clean."

The boys gladly removed or fetched their cloaks and showed them to Nikandros. They were all clean. But one cloak was missing.

"Where is your blue cloak, Leobotas?" Nikandros asked.

Leobotas's face showed just the smallest hint of panic. All of a sudden he realised that not having his cloak might be the thing that would give them away and get them into trouble. His heart started to beat faster.

"I...I don't have it," he said in a slightly trembling voice.

At this point, Lysander stepped in.

"He doesn't have it," he said, "because he lost

it saving the rest of us."

Everyone's face showed a slight surprise. Nikandros looked a little quizzical.

"How did he save you?" Nikandros asked.

"Well," without a moment's hesitation Lysander replied. "As I told you, we were collecting food in the foothills and the rough ground outside the town. There's plenty there if you know where to look. However, those hills are also home to wild boar. Unfortunately, during our foraging we disturbed a wild boar mother with her litter. She was upset and looked to charge us. Leobotas saved us by using his cloak to distract her. He tempted her to charge him by waving his cloak out in front of himself and when she got close he wrapped his cloak around her head so that she couldn't see."

Some of the boys laughed at this story as they imagined the wild boar charging off into the undergrowth with a blue cloak tightly wrapped around its head.

"We used the fact that she was blind and disorientated to escape," he continued. "So, you can see Leobotas did save us. But we don't know where his blue cloak is. It is probably still wrapped around the tusks of that wild boar and halfway up the Taygetos mountains by now."

Again, some of the boys laughed. Even though Leobotas knew the story was not true his chest swelled with pride at how heroic he had been made to appear in Lysander's story. He even felt that if things had happened the way that Lysander described them he would have done exactly as Lysander had said. He also recognised that Lysander was thinking on his feet and he admired his ability to come up with such a good story so quickly.

Lysander finished his story by adding, "....And, of course, that proves we were not at Theos Farm because if Leobotas had lost his cloak there it would be instantly recognisable. If you had found a blue cloak at Theos Farm I think you would have mentioned it straight away."

Nikandros smiled at Lysander. He knew that Lysander was lying to him because he had already spotted a small corner of the blue cloak in the embers of the fire. It was only a small piece of cloth and it was badly singed but it was unmistakably part of the blue cloak.

The fact that Lysander was lying did not matter though. The *agoge* was all about teaching the boys to fend for themselves, to think on their feet and to work together as a team. Nikandros recognised that something had changed between Lysander and Leobotas and that they were finally working as a team. This was what was important and Nikandros decided that Lysander's explanation was good enough to reassure the *ephors* that his cub pack had not been involved in the raid on the farm.

"Well done, Leobotas," said Nikandros. "I shall report to the *ephors* that it cannot have been this *paides* pack. The *ephors* will have to look elsewhere for their culprits."

Lysander shot Leobotas a quick glance, so much as to say, "*You owe me one.*"

Leobotas gave the briefest of smiles back in recognition. His eyes acknowledged the debt.

"So, that means we can return to the subject of who is to be leader," said Nikandros. "Do you all still wish Leobotas to be your leader? I imagine you are all very grateful to him for saving you from the wild boar. He has shown himself to be brave and that is an important quality in any leader. So, what do you all say?"

Leobotas decided this was the time to repay his debt to Lysander. Before the events of last night and this morning he could never have imagined himself saying this but he slowly took a step forward and in a loud voice said to Nikandros, "No, we have decided that Lysander is to be our leader and I will support him as his second in command. Lysander came up with our plan to find food last night. It worked well and we have full bellies this morning. It was he who shouted to use my cloak when the boar charged and it was he who got us back here in the dark in one piece. Lysander will be a good leader."

Nikandros smiled again. He knew that something had changed but he hadn't expected such a complete change in Leobotas as the one he had just seen.

"Is that a decision with which you are all in

agreement?" he asked.

Each of the boys nodded their approval. There was no dissent and it was clear that a sense of relief was felt in the camp.

"Very good," said Nikandros. "It is just as well that you lost the blue cloak then as we no longer have need for one. Leobotas you may now wear a red cloak along with the other boys and, Lysander, I will speak with you from time to time as the leader of this pack."

The boys congratulated each other. They patted Lysander and Leobotas on the back and there were lots of smiles all round. It felt like an important moment. The pack was finally united.

Nikandros gave them a little while to celebrate. He watched on with a smile on his face. Eventually, he raised his hand to stop their celebrations and announced, "I have one more piece of news."

The boys stopped and turned to face Nikandros.

"As I mentioned before, there is to be an athletics competition against the other *paides* and some of the girls in the *gymnasium* in one month's time. The winners will be given a special honour and the losers will be punished. I do not want this pack to lose so I will be training you hard for the next month. We will make a start today."

The boys all nodded with excitement.

XI

Gorga was as good as her word. For the rest of the day she took it easy on Helen. They did only a little simple mathematics and looked at a few Spartan poems together. As the day wore on Helen's nose hurt less and less. She began to think that perhaps her nose was not broken after all.

Towards the end of the day, Gorga turned to Helen, "I almost forgot. In the excitement of your boxing lesson this morning, I forgot to tell you about the athletics competition that is to be held in one month's time. You will be competing in a big competition in the main Arena in front of everyone. The competition will mark the start of the *gymnopaedia* festival. All the boys who have joined the *paides* this year will be there and all the girls that have started their *gymnasium* training will take part as well."

"Oh, that's exciting," said Helen. "Will Lysander be there?"

"Yes, he will," said Gorga. "But you won't be allowed to speak to him. He will stay with his *paides*."

Helen nodded. She understood. Lysander must train to be a warrior now so that he could protect Sparta and nothing could be allowed to get in the way of his training. She decided to change the subject and so asked Gorga a different question. "What events will I need to do?"

"You are fast and light," replied Gorga, "I think you will do best at the running races. That is what we will concentrate your training on. We will start tomorrow."

Helen nodded and then asked, "Will we do the *bibasis* as well?"

This question caused Gorga to pause. Helen saw a thought flash across her face. "No," replied Gorga. "The *bibasis* is a dance that is preserved for the *Karneia* festival. You will get a chance to do the *bibasis* later. But you have reminded me. Your legs were strong when we practised the *bibasis*. Perhaps you will also be good at the long jump. We will train on that, too."

Helen smiled. She liked the *bibasis* and the fact that it might make her good at something else pleased her.

"That also reminds me," added Gorga. "I have spoken to Cleitogora about you. As I mentioned, Cleitogora runs the state *bibasis* school. If you are to get a place in the state school it is Cleitogora you must impress. She is going to come with me to the athletics competition to watch you in action and see how you get on."

Helen couldn't resist. She let out a little whoop of joy and danced a few *bibasis* moves on the spot. After a little while she became calm again and, with a serious look on her face, asked, "Will I compete against the boys?"

"I don't know," replied Gorga. "Usually the

boys and the girls compete separately but sometimes, if the *ephors* think that a cub pack is weak or not trying hard enough, they will make them compete against the girls. I hope that doesn't happen to your brother's pack."

Helen nodded in agreement. She was a little disappointed though to hear that she would not be able to compete against Lysander. She felt sure that she could beat him.

"There's just one more thing," said Gorga. "Cleitogora is even harder to please than me. You will have to do really well at the competition if you are to stand any chance of getting into the state school. You will almost certainly have to win more than one event and probably will have to come out as the overall winner of the girls' competition. Are you ready for that challenge? If not, then I am not going to bother Cleitogora."

"I am ready," replied Helen. "I will make sure that I win more than any other girl. I give you my word."

At that Gorga nodded her agreement and simply said, "Good."

After Gorga left that evening, Helen's mother came over and looked at her with a concerned face. "What has happened to your nose? It looks painful."

"Gorga boxed my nose during boxing training," she admitted. "It really hurt at the time but it's less painful now."

"That's strange," said her mother. "Girls don't

usually practise boxing. Did Gorga explain why you are learning to box?"

"No," said Helen, shaking her head. "But I didn't enjoy it."

"Hmm," said her mother. "How did your ridicule song go?"

"I'm not sure," replied Helen, "Gorga didn't really say anything about it. We just went straight into the boxing after I had finished."

Demetria smiled knowingly.

"I see," she said. "I suspect that your ridicule song was good and that you hurt Gorga's feelings a little. I think that is why she decided to do boxing with you - to get her own back. That means you can be proud of your ridicule song."

Helen thought about this for a little while and began to realise that her mother might be right. Perhaps, Gorga felt a little guilty for hitting her in the face and that was why she had gone easy on her in the afternoon.

After a little while she added, "Oh, there's one other thing, Mother."

Demetria looked quizzically at Helen.

"I forgot to tell you. There is to be an athletics competition in front of the whole city. I am to compete and Lysander will be there competing as well. I am really excited about it."

Demetria squealed with joy. She exclaimed very loudly, "that means I will get a chance to see Lysander again for the first time and I will be able to see your father again. Oh this is such fantastic news Helen. Tell me all about it."

Helen explained to her mother what she knew and said that she would tell her all the details just as soon as she knew them. Demetria, of course, knew all about the *gymnopaedia* because it was an annual event in Sparta. She had just wanted Helen to tell her about it in her own words.

Both Helen and Demetria went to bed very excited that night.

CHAPTER V
The tables are turned

I

The next week was one of intensive training for the boys. Each day Nikandros arrived early. He saw to it that the boys received a good breakfast of pig's blood porridge. The boys continued to supplement this meal with extra food they foraged in the evening under Lysander's supervision. They were becoming quite good at this now. They learned where the best wild olive and fig trees were and where the best wild lemon and orange groves were. They learned not to pick all the fruit in one go but to leave a little on the tree. This encouraged the tree to produce more and so they had a steady supply of rich fruit. They learned to collect pine cones from the pine forest and how to collect the pine nuts from the cones. They learned where there were wild bee hives and how to collect just enough honey so as not to destroy the hive. They learned how to catch eels in the Eurotas by using baskets placed in the reeds.

Lysander taught them all these things and he realised that he owed Pylos a huge debt of gratitude for this. It was Pylos who had shown him how to do all these things while he had been growing up. Even though Pylos was a *helot* and Lysander was not allowed to be friends with him, his mother Demeteria had turned a blind eye and had let the boys go off together. She had thought it would be good for Lysander to have other male company given that her husband so rarely visited the house.

But it was not just Lysander who showed the boys how to get extra food. It turned out that Pausarius was quite good at stealing eggs, vegetables and loaves of bread. He explained how he knew about such things.

"When I was growing up, my family didn't have much and sometimes we went hungry. I learned to find extra food for the family. It's easy. If you find a chicken coop then there is usually a flap in the back where you can just get your hand inside. If you steal only three or four eggs then the owners don't notice. It's the same with bread. If you know when a kitchen is baking then you know that they will put out the loaves to cool down once the baking is finished. If you steal just one or two loaves the baker tends not to notice. It's the same with vegetables. If you just take one or two from a plot, the owner will not notice."

So, in this way, by using Lysander's skill at foraging and Pausarius's skill at low-level theft, the boys had a full and healthy diet. This helped enormously in their training.

II

Everyday they practised each of the disciplines that made up the Olympic Games, which were famous throughout the Greek world. Every four years, each city state in the whole of Greece sent its best athletes to compete against each other for the prize of receiving a crown made of olive leaves and having their name mentioned in poems and songs. It was also the tradition that a truce was in place during the Games. There was to be no fighting of any kind. The Olympic Games only allowed men to compete and the competition took place at a special stadium in the centre of Greece called Olympia. The Olympic stadium only allowed men to be in the audience. Some said this was because all of the competitors raced and competed naked. Even though only men were allowed in the audience it was widely known that some women did manage to get in by dressing up as men and sometimes wearing false beards. If they were caught, the women were ejected and were meant to be punished but often the authorities turned a blind eye. This was the only competition from which women were excluded. There were lots of other athletic events and festivals where they were allowed to participate.

The boys had been introduced to all the disciplines in the games before. They consisted of:

- three running races - the *stade*, which was a sprinting race, the *diaulos*, which was a middle distance race, and the *dolichos*, which was a long distance race;
- the long jump;
- the shot put;
- the discus;
- the javelin;
- boxing;
- wrestling; and
- pankration - a kind of martial arts which mixed wrestling, boxing and kicking all together. It was a very tough sport.

The boys had to train in each of the ten events. It soon became apparent though that each of them was better in one or two disciplines. This was noticed even on the second day of their training when Leobotas had tried to use the events to hurt Lysander and Ariston. Leobotas was strong and a mean fighter. He was best at the discus but he also seemed to excel at pankration and boxing. The kicks, the punches, the choke holds and the various gouges seemed to suit his style of fighting. Polydoros was tall and thin with big long legs. This made him good at the long jump. Leon enjoyed running and never seemed to get tired. He was best at the *diaulos* and the *dolichos*. The short sprint race was clearly Ariston's favourite. He seemed to have an explosive power at running that he could sustain only over a short distance. There were very few boys who could beat him at the *stade*. Charillos was able to use his weight to his advantage in the shot put. Both Lysander and Ariston were good at the javelin but Lysander seemed to have a slight advantage at the event. Pausarius had grown up in a poor household with lots of brothers and sisters. This meant he had to fight for everything both within his family and with other children who often mocked his family for being poor and so not being good Spartans. This meant that Pausarius was a natural at boxing and wrestling. That just left Teleklos. He didn't seem to be good at anything. He came in the middle of all the events. There were none that he was bad at but there were none that he excelled at. He got frustrated and disappointed by this. Lysander tried to make him feel better.

"Teleklos," he said, "I think you will be our best warrior when we grow up."

"How can that be?" asked Teleklos. "I am not good at anything."

"But you can do everything to a good standard," replied Lysander. "You may not be the best at any one event but you are the best overall because you never come last at anything. If you add up your scores from all the events you are always in the middle and that means overall your score is the highest. In battle, it will make you the most dependable warrior we have."

Teleklos smiled at this talk from Lysander. It made him feel better and he put a little bit of extra effort into his training.

III

This talk with Teleklos also placed another thought into Lysander's head. He had noticed before when they trained that each boy was better at some things than others. He decided to raise this with Nikandros at the end of the second day of training.

"Nikandros," he said. "I really want us to win the athletics competition. My mother and father will be there and I want to make them proud of me. I want them to see that I am leading a pack and that my pack is the finest in this year's *agoge*."

"What of it?" asked Nikandros.

"Well, I have noticed how some boys are better at certain events than others," explained Lysander. "With your agreement I would like those boys who are best at a particular event to concentrate their training on just that one so that they become as good at it as they possibly can be."

"But that cannot work," replied Nikandros. "The purpose of the training is to make you all fine warriors. You must, each of you, learn how to do all ten of the disciplines. These skills will stand you in good stead when it comes to battle with the Athenians or the Persians."

"I understand that," replied Lysander. "I am looking for your agreement to concentrate our training in this way just for the competition. So that we do as well as possible in front of the crowds and our families. After the competition is over we will return to training in all of the disciplines and we will give each one our very best effort. What do you say?"

Nikandros thought carefully about what Lysander was proposing. It went against all the customs and no pack had ever done this before as far as he was aware. Nonetheless, he realised that Lysander was right. If the boy that was best in a discipline concentrated their training on just that event then by the time of the competition they would be the best they could be. He also realised that Lysander had been elected as leader and that being a leader meant being clever. It meant thinking about the best way to win against your enemy and trying to out-think them as well as out-fight them.

"I think you might be right, Lysander," he said eventually. "You must not speak of it to your families or to the *ephors* but I will give you my permission to concentrate your training in the way that you have suggested."

Nikandros paused at this point. A troubled look crossed his brow and he muttered softly, almost as if speaking to himself, *"I should not speak of it."*

Nikandros's reaction began to worry Lysander. After a little while he decided to press Nikandros.

"What should you not speak of, Nikandros?" he asked.

Nikandros paused for a long time before answering. He hesitated. He cast his gaze down onto the floor. He sighed heavily. Lysander had not seen Nikandros like this before. He always seemed so composed and wise but here he was uncertain and filled with a sense of sadness. Lysander waited nervously for Nikandros to speak. Eventually he raised his head and did so.

"There is another reason why it would be good for this *paides* pack to win as many competitions as it can."

His brow went dark and Lysander began to think that he might not continue. But, at last, Nikandros went on to explain. "Each boy who fails to win an event at the *gymnopaedia* has their name written on a piece of paper and all the pieces of paper are put into a hat. The first three names that are pulled out of the hat must take part in the ceremony of the *diamastigosis*."

"What's that?" asked Lysander.

He had vaguely heard of this ceremony being mentioned in passing but he did not know any of the details of what happened during it. He could tell from Nikandros's face, however, that it must be a serious business.

"There is a reason why it is unfamiliar to you," replied Nikandros. "It is rarely spoken of in public because of what can happen at it. The *ephors* do not want to scare the new members of the *agoge*. People know that any *paides* or *paidiskoi* that does not perform well can be entered for the *diamastigosis* but they do not realise that losing at the *gymnopaedia* automatically means that your name goes into the hat. The *ephors* don't want the boys to know this because they want them to train hard for their love of Sparta not out of fear for themselves. But I know this to be true."

He paused for another moment, as if uncertain of whether he had already said too much. But then, after another shake of his head, he carried on, "It is a ceremony performed at the *limnaeon* temple in honour of the Spartan goddess *Artemis Orthia*. Those boys from the new intake to the *agoge* who are judged not to have performed well at the *gymnopaedia* must take part in the ceremony if their name is chosen. They must strip naked and walk the full length of the *limnaeon* while their fellow *paides* and *paidiskoi* line up in two opposite ranks facing each other. They then beat the boys taking part in the ceremony with sticks as they pass down the middle of the two rows. Once they make it to the altar the beating stops. The boys are often badly hurt but the intention is that they will recover in time and the experience will have toughened them up for the battlefield."

Lysander gasped, trying to take in what he had just heard.

"How harsh is the beating?" he asked eventually.

"It is harsh," replied Nikandros. "It is harsher than anything you can imagine Lysander. Any boy who is judged by the priestess not to be beating hard enough is pulled out of the line and must take the place of one of the boys being beaten. You must therefore beat your hardest. And believe me, Lysander, that is a hard thing to do when it is one of your pack that is undergoing the beating."

Lysander was shocked to hear this news.

"But it doesn't make any sense," he said. "Sparta needs all of its young men to become warriors. If young boys are beaten so harshly then they can be badly hurt or even crippled."

"Worse than that," replied Nikandros darkly. "Sometimes they can be beaten so harshly that they do not recover from their wounds."

Lysander was even more shocked.

"You mean they can die?" he gasped.

"Yes," admitted Nikandros and then after a further brief pause, he continued, "it happened to my own brother."

A tear formed in the corner of Nikandros's eye and he turned his face away from Lysander.

There was a long pause after this exchange. It was clear that Nikandros had never spoken of this before and he was greatly saddened by the memory of it. It was also clear that Lysander was shocked to learn that if his pack did not do well then, one or more of them, might end up being beaten in the *diamastigosis* and Lysander and the rest of his pack would be expected to take part in the beating.

It was Nikandros who eventually broke the silence. He wiped the tear from his eye and turned to Lysander.

"It is mainly for this reason that I have agreed with your proposal to change the training. I love Sparta and I am proud to be a Spartan but I hate the *diamastigosis* and I don't want any of you to have to experience it. I am becoming fond of this pack of *paides*. It would be good to make sure every member of it wins at least one discipline in the competition and, for your sake, your pack must be the overall victors. But you must not speak of what we have discussed. You must not mention it to your family or, more importantly, to the *ephors* because we would both be in trouble. Do you swear?"

Lysander nodded his head firmly. The idea of the *diamastigosis* deeply troubled him but this agreement with Nikandros at least gave him a chance to come up with a plan for how to avoid it.

"Good," replied Nikandros. "Let's go back to your pack and tell them about your plan."

IV

That night, as they were sitting around the campfire, after eating a hearty supper, Lysander explained his plan to the other boys. He did not mention the *diamastigosis* because he did not wish to worry them. But it was in the back of his mind all the time and so he took great effort to spell out his plan to make sure they understood the details of it and its importance to him and the pack. Each of them was excited by the prospect of just training in the things they did best because they knew that they would enjoy their training more that way and they all liked the idea of winning the competition. So, it was agreed. They would spend the rest of their training concentrating on what they were best at and helping each other to become as good as they could be in their chosen disciplines.

V

There was also one other event of note in that week of training. Half-way through the week Nikandros gathered the boys around him and made an announcement, "I have some news for you boys. Do you remember Agis, the other *paidiskoi* who is looking after another pack of *paides*? You met him briefly at the start of your training."

The boys thought for a moment and one or two of them nodded; they recalled the other teenager that Nikandros had brought with him one day. He had checked their beds and decided that Lysander's was not good enough.

"Well, it turns out that it was Agis's pack that stole the food from Theos Farm. Some of them were caught with extra food in their possession. One of them had blood on his hands where he had tried to kill a pig - it was the pig that gave the game away. As he was trying to butcher it, it squealed so loudly that it alerted the owners. When the boys' cloaks were examined carefully it was discovered that they had bits of food stuck in them. So, the *ephors* decided it must be them and they have been punished. They each received ten lashes of the beating stick on their backs. I can tell you that they looked a sorry sight when I saw them two days ago."

The boys all looked hard at the ground. They were ashamed that other boys had been punished for their actions but they were relieved that it was not them that had been caught and punished. Lysander didn't know how one of the other boys had pigs blood on his hands and how they all had bits of food in their cloaks but those had clearly been the key pieces of evidence.

Lysander began to wonder if one of the Gods had decided to help his pack. He couldn't think of another reason for this stroke of good luck.

In reality, it was because the boy had been stealing some of the pigs blood porridge before it was cooked for the rest of his pack and he couldn't admit to stealing from his own pack. The fact they had food in their cloaks was no great mystery. Like Lysander's pack they had been encouraged to steal and they had used their cloaks to carry away the things they had stolen. Nonetheless, it pleased Lysander to think that the Gods might have intervened.

"I thought you boys would be pleased to hear that," said Nikandros. "At first, people thought it was this pack but it has become clear that it must have been Agis's pack. And they made the mistake of getting caught. So their punishment is well deserved."

Nikandros knew as well as the boys that it had been them at the farm. He was congratulating them though because they had avoided being caught and that was something that was admired in Sparta.

VI

Helen's week was not dissimilar to Lysander's. Gorga was as good as her word and she concentrated Helen's training on the athletics events. Girls didn't practise boxing and pankration. So, Helen's training concentrated on the running races, the long jump, the discus and the javelin. The shot put was too heavy for Helen so Gorga quickly decided to drop that from her routine. She also decided that Helen was too light to be a good wrestler and so she dropped that from her training routine as well. Helen did enjoy making Gorga a little bit embarrassed though. When Gorga explained to her the events that women and girls did not compete in, Helen came back to the subject of boxing.

"But what about boxing? You started to teach me boxing and you hurt my nose. I wanted to get my own back. You are getting a bit old now and so I thought that I might be able to use my speed and stamina to hit you back."

"I am sorry, Mistress Helen," Gorga replied. "But girls do not often box. I am sorry about that."

"So, why did you make me put on boxing bandages and punch me in the nose?" she asked.

"I am sorry," repeated Gorga. "I let my pride get the better of me. Your ridicule song was much better than I expected and it hurt me. I was getting my own back on you. I am sorry for hurting you."

"That's alright," said Helen. "I thought as much. I forgive you. Now let's get on with my training. I want to win as many of these athletics events as I can because I want to impress Cleitogora."

Helen practised all three kinds of race but it was no surprise to find that she was best at the *dolichos* - the stamina race. Gorga had predicted this would be the case after her epic run back and forth to the Eurotas.

It turned out that Helen wasn't very good at the discus. It was slightly too big for her. Even though she could get the technique right she just couldn't get the distance. Reluctantly, Gorga decided that she would not enter Helen for the discus. Instead, she would concentrate on the javelin as her throwing discipline.

Without a doubt, however, Helen's best discipline of all was the long jump. Just as Gorga had said, Helen's bouncy, springy legs that she had used to such good effect in the *bibasis*, and her light frame, meant that she was a natural at the long jump.

The distances she achieved in that first week started to get longer and longer.

"That's amazing," exclaimed Gorga at her final jump of the week. "Your legs are as springy as a flea! I shall call you little flea!"

Even better, the use of the weights in the long jump to help the jumper gain greater distance, started to build up the strength in Helen's arms a little and her scores in the javelin also started to improve. She started off the week by throwing quite short throws but by the end of the week her throws were getting longer and longer.

Helen decided that she was enjoying her training a lot and she felt like her and Gorga now understood each other better. She was beginning to really look forward to the athletics competition. She wanted to show her mother and father that she was becoming a fine Spartan woman and that they could be proud of her. She was also looking forward to seeing Lysander again.

VII

Helen's second week of training started much the same as the first week. But then suddenly something happened to change all of that.

At breakfast, she noticed that Pylos's face was bruised and that he was avoiding her gaze. He looked worried and hurt at the same time. Helen did not have time to quiz him before Gorga arrived and so she had to spend the whole day training before she could get some time alone with Pylos.

Spartans were not really supposed to speak to *helots* unless they were giving them orders or punishing them. It was forbidden to make friends with them and even to have conversations with them. But Demetria had never been that strict about it and Helen decided that she needed to know more about why Pylos was injured.

After the evening meal she took him to one side and asked what the matter was. Pylos refused to speak to her. He shook his head violently in response to her questions and ran away at the very first opportunity.

Helen was confused. Normally, she felt that she was able to speak to Pylos and even that they got on well together. But whatever had happened to Pylos had frightened him so much that he had tightened up like a clam shell.

Helen did not want to give up so easily so she decided to speak to Pylos's mother, Lampita instead.

"Lampita," she said gently. "May I speak to you for a moment?"

Helen thought that if she asked Lampita nicely that might work better than simply giving her an order. *Helots* were very good at carrying out the instructions of an order to the letter - doing no more and doing no less. But in this case Helen needed Lampita's help.

Lampita didn't say yes but she didn't say no. She just looked at Helen in an expectant way.

"I am worried about Pylos," Helen said. "His face looks bruised and it looks like he has been in trouble. Do you know what happened to him?"

"Yes, Mistress," replied Lampita. "He was set upon by a group of boys in the market this morning. They were Spartan boys and they beat him with their fists."

"Why?" asked Helen.

"That is not for me to answer, Mistress. I am afraid that no good can come of what Pylos told me. He must tell you that story himself."

"But he's refusing to speak to me," replied

Helen. "I am worried for him. I would like to help."

"You should be worried about your brother," replied Lampita.

Lampita's face went red and she quickly looked away. She realised immediately that she had spoken out of turn. Helen looked puzzled and Lampita could see that she was going to ask more questions. Lampita waited a few moments before she spoke again.

"I am sorry for my harsh words, Mistress Helen. I did not mean to alarm you. I will tell Pylos to speak to you."

It took a little while but eventually Pylos entered the room where Helen was reading some of the poems that Gorga had given her to learn by heart.

"Come in please, Pylos," said Helen. "Take a seat, make yourself comfortable and tell me what happened to you."

Pylos sat down but he did not speak. He just looked at the ground and he looked deeply unhappy.

"Your mother says that some boys set upon you in the market," said Helen. "Why did they do that?"

"Because I am a *helot* to your family, Mistress," he replied.

"I don't understand," said Helen. "How did they know that you work for my family and why did that cause them to beat you?"

Pylos let out a loud sigh. It was clear that Helen was not going to give up until he had told her the story. He did not want to tell her what had happened because he knew that it would worry her and he was worried for his own future as well. But he realised that he was going to have to speak to her in the end. So, he took another deep breath and steadied himself before explaining everything.

"They beat me, Mistress, because I work for your family. They know that I work for your family because everyone knows about everybody's business in Sparta. It is a small place in comparison to other cities."

Helen didn't really believe that Sparta was small compared to other cities. As far as she was concerned, Sparta was the centre of the universe. But she decided not to contradict Pylos. Instead, she tried to get more information from him.

"But why did they beat you for working for my family? What have we done wrong?"

Pylos paused for a moment. He was still unsure of whether to share this information with Helen. Eventually, he decided to tell the whole story.

"They are a group of boys who will join next year's *agoge*. The brother of one of them has just joined this year's *agoge* and is in a different pack from Lysander. The boy's brother was punished by the *ephors* for stealing food from Theos Farm. But they claim they didn't do it. They believe that

Lysander and his pack did it."

"What do you mean?" asked Helen. "Lysander would never steal. He's honest. Do they think Lysander did it or someone else in the same pack as him?"

"Lysander is now in charge of his pack, Mistress," replied Pylos. "Whatever Lysander's pack does is under his orders now and so this group of boys blame Lysander for what happened to their brother."

"But how do they know all this?" asked Helen. "We haven't seen or heard from Lysander. How can they know what has happened in their brother's pack?"

"I told you, Mistress. Sparta is a small place and everybody's business is quickly known and shared by the gossips," replied Pylos.

He then paused for a few moments to let this news sink in. He could tell this was proving a difficult conversation for Helen because it was challenging a lot of her ideas about Sparta.

"Perhaps, they have broken the rules," Pylos continued. "Sometimes it is permitted for younger brothers to watch an older brother train in the *agoge*. It helps them to prepare for what will happen to them. There is not meant to be any contact between the brothers but, in this case, maybe they broke that rule. Just like you did Mistress, when you asked me to give food to Lysander while he is in the *agoge*. There is no way of knowing or proving that this is what happened but one thing I am certain of is that they are clearly angry with Lysander."

Helen's initial reaction was to be outraged that this other boy's family might have broken the rules in this way. She immediately thought about telling the *ephors*. But then her anger turned to embarrassment after Pylos's reminder that she had broken the rules herself. At first, she felt angry with Pylos for speaking to her in this way but she quickly calmed herself as she realised that Pylos was right. She couldn't really complain at others for breaking the rules if she had broken them herself.

"What can we do?" asked Helen.

"I don't know, Mistress," replied Pylos. "But there's more. After they had beaten me, they stole all the food I was carrying and left me on the ground. Another *helot* came to help me. She helped to clean my wounds a little. She gave me some milk to help get my strength back and she told me something else."

"What did she tell you?" demanded Helen.

"She told me that this was just the start of it," Pylos explained. "She said she had heard them say that they were going to beat me every time they saw me. But even worse the brother in the *agoge* is going to get his revenge on Lysander. They said something about an athletics competition and how the brother is going to make sure that Lysander will not be able to compete because they will break his bones on the day before the competition. They are planning a raid on Lysander's camp and they are going to attack him."

Helen's face dropped at this news. She was stunned into silence.

VIII

Helen was disturbed by Pylos's news all day. She couldn't concentrate on her lessons and didn't train as hard as she normally did. She kept thinking about what Pylos had told her - *a group of boys were going to raid Lysander's camp and break his bones.* The more she thought about it, the more she was worried. She waited until the evening meal and mentioned her concerns to her mother. She knew she couldn't say that she had been speaking to Pylos so decided to tell a small untruth instead.

"Mother, Gorga told me some terrible news today. Apparently, a group of boys in a different pack in the *agoge* are planning to raid Lysander's camp and break his bones so that he cannot win at the athletics competition. We have to do something to help him."

Her mother looked at her for a good while. Finally, she spoke. "It hurts my heart to hear that news, Helen. But we cannot intervene. It is part of Lysander's training and he must overcome it himself. It is learning lessons such as this that will make him strong in the field when he becomes a full Spartan warrior."

"No," said Helen. "We have to help him. He cannot learn any lessons if they sneak into his camp and break his bones."

"He must learn to deal with it himself," repeated her mother. "I absolutely forbid you from getting involved. Do you hear me?"

"Yes, Mother," said Helen in the most sulky and dejected voice she could muster.

But Helen did not agree with her mother. She made her mind up there and then that she was going to disobey her mother and that she would get a warning to Lysander in some way.

She waited until after the evening meal had been cleared away. Her mother usually went off to the main living room to do some needlework or read some Spartan poetry before going to bed. Helen asked Pylos to attend to her in her own bedroom.

"Pylos, attend to me after dinner," she said. "I feel that I need to be fully bathed. Bring plenty of hot water and sponges. I want you to give me a good clean."

"Yes, Mistress," he replied.

As soon as Pylos entered her room Helen started talking very fast in a low, hushed voice to Pylos.

"Pylos, I need your help," she said. "We cannot let those boys break Lysander's bones. I have to get a message to him to warn him. You know where Mentos Field is. I need you to draw me a map because I must go there tonight."

Pylos replied quickly. "It will be faster if I show you, Mistress. I can take you, if you will let me."

"No," replied Helen. "I cannot ask you to come with me at night. That is when the *krupteia* are about and they might kill you if they catch you."

"The *krupteia* will only kill me if they catch me alone," explained Pylos. "If I am with you Mistress, you can give me your protection. You are a Spartan and you can tell them that I am your *helot* and that they must leave me alone."

Helen nodded her agreement.

Pylos continued, "The *krupteia* are always hungry, Mistress. So if we take a little food to give to them as well that would help to make them less angry with us and they would be less likely to attack us. Shall I make up a little parcel of spare food to give them if we bump into any?"

Helen was beginning to see Pylos in a new light. She had never really considered him before. Pylos and his mother were just the *helots* that served them every day and she had never really given them any thought. But she was beginning to realise two things about Pylos. Firstly, that he was much cleverer than she had anticipated and, secondly, that he clearly cared for Lysander.

"That is an excellent idea, Pylos," Helen replied.

She wasn't too sure if Pylos caring for Lysander was a good thing. She had heard that terrible things could happen if Spartans were found making friends with a *helot*. But now was not the time to worry about that. Pylos's friendship with Lysander was clearly helpful to Helen right now and so she made a note to herself to come back to this at a later stage.

Pylos spoke up again, "If we are to go to Mentos Field this evening Mistress, then we will need to wear dark clothes so that we are not easily spotted. We should also make our faces and any bare skin as dark as possible so that we are not seen. I can use some of the embers from the cooking fire to put a layer of dark soot on our skin. That will help to make us harder to see as we move around."

"Good idea," replied Helen.

She realised again that Pylos was smart and that his help was much needed.

"When shall we go, Mistress?" asked Pylos.

"Let's wait until my mother is asleep," she replied.

And so they waited.

It seemed to take an age before Demetria fell asleep. Helen was getting impatient and her heart was pounding with excitement. She wanted to burst into the living space and make her mother go to bed straight away but she knew that would arouse suspicion.

It felt like an age but eventually Demetria

did go to her bedroom and after a short while the gentle sounds of heavy breathing and a little light snoring could be heard coming from her mother's bedroom.

This was the signal that Helen had been waiting for. She and Pylos immediately got ready to go out. They put on darker clothes and put soot on their arms and faces. Finally, they were ready.

IX

Helen was not used to being outside her home in the dark. She had been in the garden, of course, but she had never properly left the confines of her home. She hadn't realised just how scary and confusing it was to be in unfamiliar countryside when it was dark. She had no reference points to locate herself and she quickly became hopelessly lost. Her only option was to trust Pylos and to follow him in the hope that he knew where he was going. *Helots* had to follow orders at any time of day and so Pylos was used to having to fetch and carry things from many places in and around Sparta. He knew his way around well.

Helen hadn't realised how every sound or movement - even the smallest of movements - is amplified by the dark. They picked their way through the lanes and paths that crisscross Sparta and tiptoed across the patches of open ground on their journey to Mentos Field. Several times she had to fight back a little scream. She trembled at every rustling noise and shivered at every lit lamp or light shining from a house that she spotted.

Helen also hadn't appreciated just how many creatures came out at night. This played havoc with her nerves because she was expecting to bump into a *kruptoi* around every corner or hiding behind every bush. So, every time a rat scurried across their path, or a deer turned to run into the undergrowth at their approach, it made her jump.

The biggest scare of all though was when a fox caught a wild bird in its jaws. The bird fluttered its wings as fast as it could in an attempt to escape and it let out the loudest series of squawks and screeches that Helen had ever heard. She thought for one moment that a *kruptoi* must have jumped out onto the path and was murdering Pylos in front of her. It took her a few moments to realise that Pylos was in front of her unharmed and beckoning to her with his finger to his lips that she must remain silent while the noise of the fox attack was going on.

Helen felt that the fox and the bird together were making so much noise that they would awaken the whole of Sparta. She stood in horror with her heart pounding and skin breaking out into a sweat all over as she expected soldiers and others to come running out to see what was happening. She realised that if that happened then she and Pylos would be discovered and that she would be in big trouble. She also realised for the first time that if they were caught she would have to give a reason for being out after dark on her own except for the company of a *helot* boy. Her brain fought furiously for an excuse; anything that might sound plausible. But nothing came to her. She could not think of a good reason for being out on the road at night with only a single *helot*. Fortunately, for Helen she did not need to invent an excuse on that occasion. Despite all the noise of the fox and the bird no-one came out to investigate. No soldiers came running. No *ephors* appeared and, best of all, no *kruptoi* appeared. After what felt like an age of running from shadow to shadow, halting at every sound and checking carefully around every corner, Pylos dropped to his knees.

"We are here," he whispered.

Helen strained her eyes and searched for any sign of Lysander or the other boys. She could see nothing.

"Where?" she whispered back.

"They sleep over there," whispered Pylos. "Under the shadow of those trees. You won't be able to see them in the dark but they are there. I can tell."

"They sleep outside?" asked Helen.

She was shocked by this news but quickly realised that this was not the most important concern at the moment. So, she hurriedly whispered instead.

"What should we do?"

"We cannot be discovered," said Pylos. "We will need to get a little closer and wake Lysander by throwing a stone into his bedding. We must attract only his attention and we must not wake the other boys."

Helen nodded to show that she understood.

"Are you ready?" asked Pylos. "We must crawl around the outside of their camp to stay in this long grass." He paused for a few moments and then asked, "do you and Lysander have a secret way of communicating to each other? Do you have a secret sign?"

Helen thought about this for a little while.

"No, not really," she replied.

Pylos shrugged and started to crawl off into the undergrowth. For Pylos this was just another sign of how stupid the Spartans were. All *helots* communicated to each other using secret signs and language. They needed to do that so they could communicate without their masters understanding.

Helen knew she had to stay with Pylos and so she crawled behind him as quickly as she could. Pylos was obviously practised at this manoeuvre because he quickly started to go faster than her. Helen was just beginning to get to the stage where she thought she might have to call out to him because she was about to lose him when he stopped suddenly. She scrambled quickly to his side and he whispered in an even lower tone than before.

"We are here. They are just over there. Can you make out the shape of the bedding and the boys sleeping on it?"

Helen looked carefully to where Pylos was pointing. This time she could make out the dim shapes of the boys and she realised that they were a lot closer to them than she had anticipated. Her mouth started to dry up because she realised that if they made any noise at all then it could wake one of the boys and she and Pylos would be in trouble and she would bring shame on Lysander.

"I am going to throw a stone to wake him," said Pylos, gently lobbing a pebble that he found on the ground in front of them at the shape that he knew was Lysander. Helen noted with a little admiration that the throw was perfect. It landed right in the middle of the sleeping figure and it did the trick straightaway.

Before now Helen had only thought of *helots* as rather slow and stupid slaves that only did what they were told. She could tell, however, that Pylos had a lot more going for him than that.

Lysander was awakened instantly.

He sat up in his bedding and quickly scanned around to see what had disturbed him. His body was taut and rigid with tension. He reached for his *xyele* and tightened his grip around it. He expected that there might be intruders near the camp and he was ready to both give the alarm and to fight them if needed.

He quickly realised, however, that he didn't need to do that. With amazement he noticed that in the long grass only a few paces from him, Pylos was waving to him frantically with his finger to his lips to signal the need for silence.

Lysander slid quickly out of his bed. He was naked except for his loin cloth and his bare feet made no noise on the neatly swept ground. He turned quickly to check the other cubs to make sure they were still asleep and, once he had satisfied himself, he crouched down and slid into the long grass close to Pylos. When he got to Pylos he was even more amazed to see that Helen was there.

He was just about to say her name out loud when Pylos grabbed him by the head and placed his hand over his mouth.

"Shhh," Pylos whispered with the faintest of sounds - barely even a noise at all.

He beckoned to Lysander to follow them and he started to crawl back to the place where they had first arrived at the camp.

Finally, when Pylos considered that they were out of hearing distance of the other boys, he stopped and said in a low hush, "We can talk here."

Lysander didn't know where to begin. He wanted to hug Helen, tell her and Pylos off for being out at night on their own and ask them why they were there. He decided to leave the hugging for last and so asked them, "What are you doing here? You have taken such a risk. I can't believe it."

Helen was the one who answered. "We had to see you," she said. "To warn you that you are going to be attacked by a group of other cubs in the *agoge*. I don't know what you have done to them. Something about stealing from a farm. Their relatives attacked Pylos when they found out he worked for our family and they made threats saying they are going to cripple you, Lysander, on the day before the competition so that you cannot win at the athletics."

It took a moment for all this to sink in, but once it had, Lysander slowly nodded his understanding.

"That must be the *paides* who were punished for the raid on Theos Farm. They think that was me - but it wasn't. Thank you so much for the warning. I will be on my guard from now on."

And with that he gave first Helen and then Pylos a massive hug to say thank you and to show them how much he appreciated what they had done for him.

It took a few moments for Helen to process what had just happened but then she realised with a sense of shock that Lysander had just hugged Pylos in front of her. If anyone else had seen that it would mean instant death for Pylos and never-ending shame for Lysander.

She looked around and realised that it was completely dark around them and no-one else could see. She felt relieved but realised that she would need to give more thought later to what she had just witnessed.

Lysander interrupted her thoughts, "I cannot tell you how grateful I am to you both for what you have done," he said. "But it is very dangerous for you both to be out here. You must return to the house now. I will see you again Helen at the athletics competition. Make sure you bring Pylos with you as your *helot*. Armed with what you have told me tonight I will make sure that the other cub pack does not succeed. Thank you again."

Helen realised the truth of Lysander's words and she reluctantly agreed to leave him and make the journey back. Lysander returned to his bed to consider his next steps.

X

He was incredibly grateful to both Helen and to Pylos for the risk that they had taken to bring him this news. However, this revelation now created a new problem for him and the turmoil this caused meant that he had a sleepless night. He spent most of it turning over this problem in his mind. His single thought was *what should I do?*

His first dilemma was whether to tell the

other boys about the news or to keep it to himself. He wanted to keep it quiet because he couldn't think of a good explanation for how he had received the news. So, he considered keeping it to himself and trying to deal with the problem alone. The more he thought about it, however, the more he realised that he could not take on a whole pack of *paides* by himself and that he would need the help of his own *paides* if they were to triumph. So, he decided that he must share the news in the morning. His next problem was to explain how he had received the news. He knew that he could not say that his sister and a *helot* boy had visited him in the night. That would mean only one thing - punishment for them all and Lysander's removal as leader of the *paides*. No, he decided, he had to find a way of explaining how this had happened without telling the truth.

He thought long and hard about this. Could he have heard a rumour that the other boys didn't hear? Not really because he had not spent any time away from the rest of the boys. Could Nikandros have told him? Again, no. Nikandros would quickly deny this. He had to come up with a different explanation. He tossed and he turned in his bed. No matter how much he thought about the problem or how hard he tried, an answer would not come to him. Eventually, he started to become so tired that he drifted off into a restless half sleep. He started to have a dream that he was back home with his mother and his sister. He dreamt of himself wrapped up in bed with a bowl of warm milk and his mother sitting on the edge of his bed telling him a story in that soft, soothing voice she used to calm him and Helen at bed time.

He half-remembered in his dreams a jumble of some of the stories that his mother had told him. He remembered that she had told him that the Spartans were a religious people - the most religious people in the whole of Greece. He remembered that she had told him many stories about the Gods and their exploits. Snippets and snatches of these stories came to him in his dreams. He remembered many of the things that Zeus had done. Zeus was the father of all the Gods and was the most powerful of them all. He remembered a story about one of Zeus's sons, Apollo. Apollo was, among other things, the Greek God of prophecy and Lysander remembered several stories about how Apollo had chosen to help special humans by giving them a vision of the future. Lysander's mother had said that to be visited by Apollo was considered a great honour and a sure sign that the person visited was destined for great things. He also remembered his mother's stories about Ares, another son of Zeus. Ares was the Greek God of war. He was said to look out for Greeks in times of war and protect their best warriors from harm. He remembered his mother telling him that Ares was said to have a special place in his heart for Spartans. He smiled on the Spartans and was, in part, responsible for many of their great victories. As he remembered these dreams the faces of Apollo and Ares came to him and they moved in and out of his consciousness. Eventually, he realised that their faces had merged in his dreams into a single face. A single face that was familiar to him and which comforted him in his turmoil. That face was the face of his father. He remembered his father's three rules - form a strong bond with the other members of your pack, put the needs of the group above the needs of yourself and never feel self-pity. And then in his half-dream, half-awake state he heard his father speak to him loudly and clearly. He heard him speak in words that pierced his heart.

"When faced with a problem, Lysander, always choose the Spartan way."

And that was it. Lysander suddenly knew what to do. He was ready for action.

XI

As soon as the boys awoke the next morning Lysander called them together.

"We have a problem," he explained. "I have received news that the boys from Agis's pack are planning to attack us and injure us so that we cannot win the athletics competition. We have to decide how we will stop them."

The boys were a little taken aback by this news. Charillos was a little scared because he knew that this probably meant fighting and he didn't really like fighting. He knew he had to become a warrior but he was secretly hoping to find another way to serve Sparta. This news meant he was not going to be able to avoid fighting.

Leobotas, however, thought about what Lysander had said and he had a question. "How did you get this information?"

He didn't ask this in a malicious way. It was clear that he was not trying to trap Lysander. He was genuinely curious because he had spent the whole day with Lysander the previous day and knew that he had not met anyone else.

Lysander was ready for this question. He spoke loudly and confidently. "The Gods told me in my sleep. Apollo and Ares visited me. Apollo told me that for the good of Sparta I must protect my *paides* and that we must vanquish all at the athletics competition. Ares told me that we will all become great Spartan warriors in time but our first challenge is to overcome the fellow Spartans who seek to do us harm."

The boys stood in awe. For one or two of them their jaws literally dropped and they stood there open mouthed. For a Spartan not only did Lysander's story make perfect sense it also meant that they as a *paides* were chosen ones - being looked after by the Gods. They felt a huge sense of pride and pleasure in this news of Lysander's dream. It meant a lot to them.

It took a little while for the shock and joy of this news to wear off. But eventually Ariston snapped out of it and started to ask questions. "What must we do? When will they attack us? How do we defend ourselves?"

Lysander smiled to himself. He knew his story had had the desired impact. The other cubs were with him and they wanted to work together. Putting on his most serious face he addressed them again. "These are excellent questions, Ariston," he said. "I have been giving this a lot of thought since the Gods left me. I am told that Agis's pack will attack on the day before the athletics competition. I am sure that they will come under the cover of darkness and we must be prepared. We must set a trap for them."

"What kind of trap?" asked Leobotas, who was clearly excited about the prospect of a fight.

"All in good time, Leobotas," Lysander said. "Let me explain my plan. It has three stages to it."

The boys all nodded in anticipation. Lysander gestured to them to sit around him in a circle while he explained the plan. The boys happily sat to listen.

"Firstly," Lysander said. "We must set a watch during the night so that they do not take us by surprise. I will ask Leobotas to draw up a rota and each boy will stay awake for one hour during the night to spot whether we are about to be attacked. If nothing happens during his awake period he will wake the next boy and he will do the same and so on until dawn. We will start this watch two nights before the competition - just in case they decide to come early."

The boys did not like the idea of being woken but they realised quickly that Lysander's plan made sense and so none of them complained. Ariston was following every word that Lysander said and he had a question at this point.

"How will we tell the time during the night, Lysander?" he asked. "We do not have an hour candle."

"That is a good question, Ariston," replied Lysander. "It is another sign that the gods have favoured us. The night before the athletics competition will be the night of the full moon. When the moon is full it is bright and we can set up a gnomon, just like we would do in the daytime."

Ariston nodded his agreement. He was happy to trust Lysander on this matter.

"May I continue with the rest of the plan now please?" asked Lysander.

Ariston nodded enthusiastically.

"Secondly," continued Lysander. "We must not sleep in our beds on the night of the attack. We will leave our beds here and we will make dummies of ourselves out of sticks and reeds that we will put under our cloaks to make it look like we are asleep. In that way, Agis's pack will attack our dummies and not us. We will sleep under the shade of those olive trees. We will make small hollows in the ground that we will sleep in and we will cover ourselves with leaves so that we cannot easily be seen in our beds."

The boys liked this part of the plan much better. It felt like a good deception of the kind that the Spartans were famous for. Pausarius even liked the idea of sleeping in a hollow in the ground. He had slept like that before and he found it comfortable.

"Finally," said Lysander. "We will train ourselves to fight as a phalanx."

He paused for effect.

"What's a phalanx?" asked Charillos.

"It is the military formation that Spartans use in battle," replied Lysander. "It is what Spartans use to strike the fear of the Gods into their opponents."

The boys all nodded with approval. This was the advice his father had given him.

"Nikandros has not started our military training yet and so we must teach ourselves," Lysander continued. "We have all read the poems of Tyrtaeus about the power of the phalanx and we have all seen the pictures on plates and beakers. We will train ourselves to fight in this manner to defend ourselves for when Agis's pack arrive."

"But we do not have our own *xystons*," said

Teleklos.

Lysander thought back to the huge eight foot spear that his father had shown him that would be his. He had called it a *xyston* and Lysander quickly realised that is what Teleklos was referring to.

"No," he agreed. "We do not have a *xyston* and we are still too small to use one properly. But we shall make our own *xystons* - ones that are more suited to our size. Also, we will not place spear tips on them as we do not want to kill our enemy on this occasion. We merely want to stop them."

He paused to let this information sink in. The boys were clearly excited by the idea but confused about how to put it into practice. After all, there were not a lot of spare *xystons* lying about.

"I know a place where silver birch trees grow in abundance," Lysander continued. "Young silver birch grow straight and thin and will make excellent shafts for our *xystons*. We can cut them and plane them with our *xyele*. Once we have made them we can hide them in our beds so that Nikandros does not see them."

XII

And so, that is what the pack did. They spent the day training with Nikandros and after he had left for the evening they went out to cut and fashion their own *xyston*. The next day after that they made their new beds under the olive trees and fashioned the dummies that would fool the attackers into thinking that they were asleep. They hid the dummies in their hollow beds and then camouflaged them until they would be needed in a few days' time. The next evening after that, Lysander started to train them in how to use their *xystons*. The key was to work together in unison. The phalanx stood tightly together, shoulder to shoulder. When the leader shouted "strike" they all struck together in unison. In that way the enemy was faced with a wall of blows all coming at the same time. He could defend against one, or if he was good, against two but he could not defend against all the blows coming in at the same time.

Lysander spent a week training his pack in this way. By day they trained for the athletics event. Each of them concentrating on the events that they did best and getting better and better all the time. By night they trained in the manoeuvres of the phalanx. They became good at this, too. By the end of a week they could move and turn as a single unit and when Lysander shouted "strike" they each thrust their *xyston* forward with maximum force.

They practised like this every evening until two days before the day of the athletics competition. At that point they put into practice the system of being awake to spot the intruders sneaking into the camp.

They were a little disappointed after the first night when no-one came which meant that there was only one night left for the attack to come.

XIII

Agis's pack waited until Agis had left them for the evening. At that point, the leader turned to the other boys with grim determination on his face.

"Right, it is time to get revenge for the beating that the *ephors* gave us because of Lysander and his *paides*. Let's hurt them as much as the *ephors* hurt us. Let's also make sure that they cannot win the competition tomorrow. Are you all ready? Take a stick each to beat them in their beds. I will take a hammer to break one of Lysander's legs. That will teach him a lesson he will not forget."

The other members of Agis's pack signalled their agreement. They equipped themselves and started to move out under the cover of darkness.

The *paides* camps were kept far apart so that the boys did not bump into each other by accident. Agis's pack moved swiftly, however, and so they reached Lysander's camp quickly. At the point they arrived, their leader signalled to them all to stop, go down on one knee and rest for a few moments to get their breath back. The full moon was bright and they could see the reed beds in the corner of the open field. It was clear that the boys were asleep on them as their cloaks clearly outlined the shape of their bodies.

When they were all rested he whispered to his pack.

"Alright, spread out and take one each. Beat them good with your sticks. I want to see them covered in blood and bruises."

XIV

It was Leon who was on guard duty in Lysander's camp when the attack started. He was sitting in the branches of one of the olive trees so that he was a little higher up. This gave him a good view across the camp ground. It also meant that he was hidden from view and quickly spotted the intruders as they arrived. He gently whistled to the other boys as softly as he could.

"They are here. Get ready."

Each boy's body stiffened in its little hollow bed. Each of them firmed their grip tightly on the *xyston* that was lying in the hollow with them. They were ready and they were coiled for action.

Leon watched the intruders run into the camp. They reached the dummies under the cloaks and prepared to rain down blows on them. As the first blow was about to fall, Leon jumped down from the tree.

"Lysander, you're in command," he shouted.

Lysander sprang up, as did all the other boys.

"Phalanx, form a line on me!" he shouted.

Then as soon as the line was formed he shouted again.

"Advance to contact!"

The boys of Agis's pack were completely surprised. They did not really know what was happening.

One moment they were about to beat with all their might the bodies that they thought were on the ground. The next they were faced with a line of boys all standing in unison and armed with long spears. One or two of them tried to attack the phalanx with their sticks but they could not get near. They were faced with a hail of blows that went into their chests and stomachs. From the sound of cracking it was clear that more than one set of ribs was broken.

The only one who put up any resistance was the leader of Agis's pack. He was the one who was armed with the hammer and he made straight for Lysander. His face was red with fury and he clearly meant to hurt Lysander as badly as he could. He gave the hammer a huge swing at Lysander's head. Lysander saw the blow. He used his own *xyston* to parry the blow so that it did not hit him. The two boys to the left and right of him still thrust their *xystons* forward and hit the other leader with all their might. One blow went straight into his chest and winded him. The other smashed into his face and caught him full on the nose. There was a loud crack of bone and gristle as his nose was flattened by the blow.

He dropped the hammer and shrieked in pain. He looked around him and saw that his whole pack was in full flight. They were all running off, shrieking with pain and fear. He turned on his heels and followed his pack. His eyes were full of tears. He knew that he had lost and that his pack could not compete at the games tomorrow and win.

Lysander's pack let out a huge cheer.

"We've done it!" cried Leobotas. "We have defeated them!"

"Yes," replied Lysander. "You were all fantastic. This is a famous victory. Apollo and Ares will be proud of us."

There was general excitement and congratulations in the camp for some time. The boys had joined the *agoge* in order to learn to work together as a unit and to fight for the survival of Sparta. It felt like they had just had their first really big lesson in how to do that. Lysander decided to let the boys enjoy their victory and celebrate a little. Eventually, however, he paused them. "Let's get some sleep now," he said. "Our victory tonight is only half the task. The next thing we must do is win the competition tomorrow!"

CHAPTER VI
The athletics competiition

I

Finally, it arrived. The morning of the athletics competition. Lysander did not completely understand why but he was incredibly nervous. He knew that it was a personal test and that he must win his event. He also knew it was a public test of his leadership and of his whole pack. But more than that, he saw it as a private test. He did not want any of his pack to have to undergo the *diamastigosis* and he saw it as his own private challenge to ensure that this did not happen. His group had to succeed as a whole as well as individually if he himself was to avoid the *diamastigosis*. This meant that Lysander felt an immense weight on his shoulders. He felt that he had done as much to prepare for this outcome as possible but, nonetheless, he had spent another night of fitful sleep. He had kept turning his plans over in his mind to reassure himself that he had done the right thing. He realised it was too late to change things now but he couldn't stop worrying and turning things over in his mind.

He was sure of one thing. He didn't want any of his *paides* to come away without a win. He did not want any of them to have their name put in the hat for the *diamastigosis*. He could not bear the thought of them being beaten, or worse, he himself having to take part in the beating. He thought about his father's advice again:

"*Make friends with the other members of the pack.*" Well, he had done that and he was now their leader.

"*Always put the needs of the group above the needs of yourself.*" He was thinking about his group and not about himself.

"*Never feel self-pity.*" He was not feeling self-pity. He was consumed with a steely determination to protect his pack.

So, for the first time since he had left home, he realised that his father's advice was of no help to him. It provided no guidance.

He knew that this was a problem that only he could solve. So, he had spent another long night tossing and turning as he carefully went through in his mind his plan to ensure that every member of the pack came away with at least one victory.

He was confident about Leobotas. He was a strong boy who liked fighting. He was sure that Leobotas would win either at the wrestling, the boxing or the pankration. He was also good at the discus. So, there was no need to worry about Leobotas.

For the same reason he was confident about Pausarius. Pausarius had had a hard life and he was a born fighter, too. Lysander knew that he would also do well in at least one of the fighting disciplines.

He was equally confident about Leon. Leon seemed a natural runner and Lysander was sure that Leon would win either the *dolichos*, the *diaulos* or even both.

Lysander was reasonably confident about Ariston. He was a quick runner over short distances and Lysander felt he had a good chance at winning the *stade*.

But he was less sure about Polydoros. He seemed best suited to the long jump and that is what he had trained in. He thought Polydoros had done well in training but he was not fully confident that there couldn't be someone better than him in another pack.

The two he was least confident about were Charillos and Teleklos. Charillos seemed to have a natural gift for the shot put but he was such a clumsy boy that you couldn't be confident that he would perform well on any given day. Lysander decided that he must put a special effort into supporting Charillos today to ensure that his mind was in the right place and that he concentrated on the task at hand.

Teleklos was also a problem. He wasn't bad at anything but he wasn't good at anything either. Lysander just couldn't see where Teleklos was going to get a victory. He thought that, on balance, the running events or the discus might be his best chance. So, Lysander had decided to enter Teleklos into the long jump, the *dialochos*, the sprint and the discus. Lysander thought this was the best plan he could come up with for Teleklos. Teleklos had tried really hard in training for all four events and was improving in all of them. Lysander was still not confident of success for him though.

That just left Lysander himself. Where was he going to get a victory? He was sure that his best event was the javelin. He had trained hard at it and he was getting really good throws. So, he decided that was where he should put his maximum effort.

II

It was for all of these reasons that Lysander's stomach was tight as a knot and he had to force himself to eat his breakfast. He knew that his body needed the fuel to perform at his best but his nerves meant that he felt no sense of hunger at all.

Lysander didn't know it but every single boy in his pack felt the same. None of them knew about the *diamastigosis* but they all wanted to do well in front of their families. They had trained hard and had many bruises and cuts to show for it. They had even fought off an attack the previous night and, even though they didn't fully appreciate it, they had used the perfect tactics of a Spartan warrior to defeat their opponents.

If Nikandros had seen them he would have been incredibly proud of them. They all knew, however, that they must not speak of last night and that their victory must be a secret.

So, the camp that morning was quiet. The boys went about their business in silence. They did not speak to each other or pay each other much attention. They made sure they washed and cleaned themselves so that they looked at their best. Their hair had begun to grow a little now since they had joined the *agoge* and they started to clean and fashion it as best as they could.

It was a little bit the same in Helen's house. Yet different at the same time. Helen also woke up nervous because she wanted to succeed for herself and to show that she could perform as well, if not better, than any of the other girls in her age group. She was also nervous because, if Gorga was as good as her word, the woman who ran the state *bibasis* school would be there to watch her. Whether she would gain entry to the state school would depend on how well she did today. But she was also nervous because she did not know what had happened to Lysander. She and Pylos had been incredibly brave in taking a risk and going off to warn Lysander but she had no idea whether her warning had been of any use.

As far as Helen knew, her brother could be lying with his bones broken right now and he could be in terrible pain. So, she didn't know whether she would see him or not. And if she did see him she still did not know what to do or say to him about that embrace she had seen him give Pylos. Under all the laws of Sparta what had been done was illegal and should be punished by the *ephors*. In fact, by not telling the *ephors* she herself was committing a crime which could get her into trouble.

All these things were going around in her mind. The result was that she was just as worried and anxious as Lysander but her reasons were different ones.

III

By chance Lysander and Helen both arrived at the stadium for the competition at around the same time. They both stood open mouthed for a moment as they took in the scene before them. They couldn't believe it. It felt like the whole of Sparta was here. The noise was incredible. People were chatting loudly, they were moving around as they arrived to take their place in the crowd and everyone was jostling for space and the best view. There were flags and banners fluttering from the walls of the stadium and from flag poles erected especially for the event. These all flapped in the breeze giving an impression of great movement adding to the spectacle of the people in motion. There were *helots* everywhere making and handing out food to the Spartan spectators. Musicians played flutes, lyres and cymbals. The noise was deafening and simply added to the nervousness and anxiety that all the participants felt.

The stadium was an oval in shape and the crowd sat around the outside in big banks of seating upon stone steps that increased in height the further back they went from the games area. In the middle was the running track which went all the way around in a huge oval inside the area just in front of where the seating began. Inside the running track were a series of areas marked out for the throwing and jumping events. Finally, in the middle, on a slightly raised podium, was the fighting area for the boxing, the wrestling and the pankration. This was also the place where the victors would be awarded their laurel wreaths. Laurel wreaths were awarded in honour of Apollo at the *gymnopaedia* rather than olive wreaths.

What caught both Lysander's and Helen's attention most of all, however, were the pendants that separated the area between the running track and the seating into five distinct zones within the stadium. Above each zone fluttered a huge pendant which announced - **Paides Nikandros**, **Paides Agis**, **Paides Dienakes**, **Paides Nabis** and **Girls of the Gymnasium**.

They both realised these must be the zones where they would sit during the contest when they were not competing. This is where they would be given food, water and medical care if they needed it.

Lysander pointed to the pendant with Nikandros's name on it and directed his pack to that area to go and sit and prepare for the event to begin. As they approached the pendant he was a little surprised to see in small writing underneath the main headline of **Paides Nikandros**, the words *Lysander, son of Leon and Demetria*.

When he got to the area marked out for him he was even more surprised to see, sitting in the seating behind him and near the front row, his mother and father, Demetria and Leon. They both let out a big cheer as he approached them and gave him a huge wave.

"Come on, Lysander," his father shouted. "Do Sparta proud today!"

He acknowledged the shout with a weak smile and a little wave of his own. He realised that other members of his pack were also giving small waves or smiles to other people in the audience. These must be the parents of his fellow pack members he reflected to himself. He started to recognise one or two faces of the men who had accompanied their sons on that first morning when they all entered the *agoge* together.

Lysander also looked about him at his fellow competitors - the other boys in the other packs. He watched them carefully as they started to assemble. He watched how they handled themselves, how they interacted with each other and whether they looked nervous or not. He did not see anything that gave him cause to worry except he noted that in the **Paides Dienakes** there was one boy who stood out. He was much bigger than all the others. He looked almost big enough to be a teenager but Lysander knew that he could not be. *He will be difficult to fight,* Lysander thought to himself, *he is probably going to give us the most trouble.*

Lysander also noticed that no boys seemed to be assembling in the area marked out for **Paides Agis**. It seemed that the reception that he and his pack had given them the night before had been enough to knock the competition out of them. Lysander had mixed emotions about this. On the one hand, he was pleased that he had saved himself and his pack from physical harm. On the other, he was worried that the Agis boys might tell Agis what had happened to them and that Lysander's pack might get into trouble with the *ephors*.

He was also worried that if they were not present their names could not be put into the hat for the *diamastigosis*. This meant that if Lysander's pack failed then the chances of their names being in the hat were increased. He shuddered at the thought.

What Lysander did not know was that many of the Agis boys were too badly injured to compete that morning. As a result, Agis had forbidden them from coming so as to avoid the public humiliation of being seen to be covered in bruises and with broken ribs. He knew they were in no fit state to compete and he also wanted to avoid the shame of his pack coming last in every competition. He had told the organisers of the competition that his pack were ill with food poisoning - bad pigs blood porridge - and that they could not compete. He had pressed his pack to tell him what had happened but they would not speak. The shame of losing was too great and all they would say was that someone had invaded their camp and beaten them in their sleep. Agis did not believe them as there were no signs of a struggle in or around their camp. But his boys would not say anything different to him.

That meant that the boys' competition only involved boys from three packs rather than the expected four. But there wasn't much time for Lysander to dwell on the absence of Agis's pack. His parents kept trying to catch his eye and shout things to him. He was aware that the other parents were doing the same thing. He wanted them to stop so that he could concentrate on the competition and collect his thoughts.

His thoughts were interrupted again, however, as an *ephor* came over to his pack and started to take the names, the dates of birth and the parents' names of each of the boys in the pack. This was the first time that any of the boys had seen an *ephor* close up. They had expected the *ephor* to be a young fit warrior but it was clear, however, that this man was not young.

When Lysander looked around the stadium and saw the other *ephors* he realised that none of them were young men. They were all older men with grey hair and, in many cases, they were either bald or becoming bald. What they lacked in youth, however, they made up for in sternness. Each of them had a steely look in their eyes and a short, clipped manner in their speech. They gave the impression that it would take only one wrong word or one small mistake to set them off and incur their wrath. Each of them carried on their belt a long staff with a head that bulged out into a club-like end. It was clear that this was their beating staff. Lysander got the impression that it would take only one mistake to make the *ephor* detach the club from his belt and put it to good use.

IV

Helen walked towards the area marked out for the Girls of the Gymnasium. She noted with some frustration that the pendant for her area did not carry her name. She had spotted, even with the small writing, that Lysander's pendant carried his name and she thought to herself how unfair it was that a boy could get his name in writing but the girls were anonymous. She was still nervous but this small injustice angered her a little and fired her up with even more determination to prove herself. She also noted that her parents did not seem to be here. She looked long and hard but she could not see them in the crowd anywhere near the section where she was stationed. Eventually, however, she did spot Gorga in the crowd. She was sitting in the section near to her but much further back. Next to Gorga was a woman that Gorga was in animated conversation with. Helen guessed that this woman must be Cleitogora, the woman who ran the state *bibasis* school. Indeed, without waving or acknowledging Helen's presence, it became clear to Helen that Gorga was pointing her out to the other woman and they were talking about her. She swallowed her pride and her anger a little and she waved to Gorga to acknowledge her presence. Gorga did not respond and seemed to ignore Helen. It was only when she saw a little wave from someone a short distance to the side did she realise that Pylos was there to act as the *helot* serving Gorga and Cleitogora. Helen knew that she could not be seen waving to Pylos, so she just gave him a tiny smile. It was the smallest flicker of a smile that she could get away with. It was so small that anyone who did not know her would not recognise that she was smiling. But it was enough for Pylos to recognise it. He gave her a small smile in return.

Helen was also relieved because, once the boys had assembled in the area marked out by their pendant, she could see that Lysander was with them. She noticed that one of the other areas marked out for a pack was not being occupied. So, she realised that her warning must have had its effect.

She wanted to catch Lysander's eye to show him that she was pleased that he was safe but he was on the other side of the arena and there was too much going on around him for her waves or shouts to be heard. She also noted with a small amount of disappointment that her parents were in the crowd behind Lysander. They had chosen to sit with him and not her. In other circumstances, this example of another injustice against girls would have made her angry. Because she was nervous, however, she simply noted it and shrugged it off.

So, instead, Helen sat herself down and started to prepare for the games that were shortly about to begin. She could see that Lysander was doing the same. She saw that he was seated in the area marked out for him and that he had put his red cloak over his head so as to block out all the movement and noise around him. She thought this was a good idea and she wished she had a cloak like that so that she could do the same thing.

Instead, she started to look at her own competition. There were now seven other girls sitting in the same area as her. She realised these must be her competitors. She took comfort from the fact that they all looked as nervous as she felt. Helen eyed each one of them up carefully and noted that they all looked fit, healthy and strong. There were no obvious small, overweight or weak ones among them and she decided that this was going to be a tough competition. There was also something about one of the other girls that unnerved her.

They looked nervous or scared and they were looking mainly at their parents or relatives in the crowd or were just staring at the ground. There was one girl, however, whose gaze did not move. It was fixed forwards and was unflinching. This girl was obviously preparing herself and concentrating only on the competition to come. There was something about the girl that Helen did not like the look of - she made her uneasy.

V

Everyone's thoughts and conversations were suddenly interrupted by a series of loud blasts from three trumpets. Everyone knew that this heralded the start of the games.

First, the *ephors* marched into the centre of the stadium. They lined up and took out their beating sticks. Then a man dressed in full Spartan armour marched into the arena. He stood in front of the *ephors* and in their turn they raised their beating sticks above their heads and simultaneously let out a loud cry. "All hail, the Kings of Sparta."

The crowd rose in unison and replied with a single voice. "All hail, the Kings of Sparta."

The noise was deafening and suddenly the atmosphere in the stadium changed. Gone was all the chit chat and the moving about. The crowd became silent and still. There was a sense of expectation that rippled through them like the shock you get when you grab a young electric eel by its tail. The effect on all the boys and girls was as if their spines had been turned into staffs.

They had been nervous before but now their every sense jingled and jangled with expectation. They felt their hearts beating and their blood pumping through their veins. It was the scariest moment of each and every one of their lives.

The warrior turned to face the crowd. He removed his helmet and his hair fell about his shoulders in tight braids. Raising his voice he addressed the crowd. "People of Sparta, I am Cleomenes. I am the emissary of King Aristodemos, the Europontid King of Sparta. Next year this honour will pass to the Agaid King. But this year, King Aristodemos is proud to sponsor the annual *gymnopaedia*."

He paused and a blast of the three trumpets rang out again. In response to this the crowd stood and shouted once more, "All hail

Aristodemos, the Europontid King of Sparta."

Cleomenes waited for the cries to die down and then he continued, "King Aristodemos is proud to sponsor this annual event. It is a most important day in the whole of the Spartan calendar. It is the day we come together to welcome the new members of the *agoge*. The very future of Sparta is gathered in this stadium and we come to see their potential and to give them our best wishes for their future and for the future of Sparta."

Again, he paused and again there followed three blasts of the trumpet. The crowd rose to their feet and shouted in the loudest possible voice, "All hail, the future of Sparta."

Cleomenes waited a moment and then he motioned to the crowd by raising both his arms and lifted them to the sky with his palms turned upwards to face the sun. The crowd recognised the meaning of his gesture instantly and they bellowed again. "All hail, the future of Sparta!"

Cleomenes repeated this gesture twice more. At the end of this ritual the crowd had been whipped up into a fury and the atmosphere in the stadium was palpable. You could almost taste the excitement and the energy. Cleomenes spoke once more. "In accordance with Europontic tradition we will begin the games with a short reading of Spartan poetry by the great poet, Tyrtaeus, the national poet of Sparta. This reading will be given by the *paidiskoi* chosen by the *ephors* as the pack that has trained the hardest and which is most likely to succeed as warriors. *Ephors*, have you chosen a *paidiskoi* to read to us?"

The chief *ephor* took a step forward and spoke loudly. "We have. This year's *paidiskoi* reader will be Nabis."

Nabis beamed a broad smile and brushed himself down as he walked towards the lectern in the centre of the stadium where he would read the poetry aloud.

Lysander gulped. If Nabis had been chosen then that meant that his pack must be the best. Perhaps all Lysander's carefully thought out plans to avoid the *diamastigosis* were about to fall apart... Lysander felt a sense of panic and dread start to rise in his stomach. He began to give the boys sitting under the Nabis flag a second look. He stared hard but he couldn't get a clear look at them as they were all celebrating and congratulating each other over the fact that Nabis was the reader. Lysander began to feel very worried.

As Nabis stepped onto the podium a *helot* handed him a book opened at the appropriate page. Clearing his throat he began to read outloud. He spoke slowly and in a loud clear voice so that all could hear.

"For no-one ever becomes a man good in war
unless he has endured the sight
of blood and slaughter,

> stood near, and lunged for the foe.
> This is virtue, the finest prize
> achieved among human kind,
> the fairest reward that a young
> man can carry off.
> This is a common good, shared by
> the entire city and people,
> when a man stands his ground,
> remains in the front ranks.
> This is a man who's become good in war."

As soon as Nabis had finished, the crowd stood again and shouted, "All hail, the future of Sparta."

There was no doubt in anyone's mind about the meaning of the words. They were an instruction to the new boys of the *agoge* on what was expected of them both in battle and in life. Their introduction to the Spartan army had begun several weeks ago when they entered the *agoge*. But today it became real for them. They understood the expectation that everyone shared about what they must do and how they must do it.

The boys looked at each other and nodded their understanding and grim determination. Lysander gathered them around him and spoke to them so that only they could hear him.

"Right boys, we know what it's like to stand in the phalanx from last night. We have trained hard for this moment. We are ready. Let's do this!"

They pumped their fists in agreement.

The noise of the crowd could still be heard loudly. Everyone was excited for what was to come.

CHAPTER VII
The long jump

The long jump was announced as the first event. The boys would begin and the girls would follow. For the boys' event, each pack was invited to put forward their three best members to compete. For the girls' event all the girls present took part.

In accordance with his plan, Lysander nominated Polydoros (his best), Ariston and Teleklos to compete for his pack. Each boy had three jumps and only his longest jump counted and would win the competition. For the jump to count, the boy had to take off from behind a line on the jump board. If his foot strayed over the line then he would get a black flag and the jump would not count. If his foot was behind the line he would get a white flag and his jump would be measured. If his jump was the longest that day then he would be the winner. The competition was close. Polydoros was clearly nervous. He failed his first two jumps, receiving two black flags. At the end of the second round of jumps it was Ariston who had made the best one but he was quite a way behind the best jumper from **Paides Nabis.**

Lysander was worried about two things. Firstly, he knew that Polydoros could win. He had seen him jump further in training but the roar of the crowd and the atmosphere were clearly affecting him. If Lysander couldn't find a way to calm Polydoros down and get him to perform at his best then he could lose and, worse, be forced to undergo the *diamastigosis*. Secondly, it was only the first event and already **Paides Nabis** were beginning to look really strong. He was worried they might sweep the board and win at everything. Just before his final jump, Lysander took Polydoros aside and whispered to him. "This is it, Polydoros. I have every confidence in you. I know that you are the best jumper here. You have jumped much better than this in training. Show this crowd what you can do."

Polydoros went to the start of his run. He took the lead weights in his hands and he ran forwards. He ran as fast as he could and he thudded into the jump board with all his might. His feet landed solidly on the board rather than in front of it and he sailed through the air. Throwing the weights behind him just at the right time he gained the extra little bit of momentum that this provided. His jump was long. At least two hands length further than the best jump so far. He landed and immediately looked backwards to the *ephor* who was checking where his feet had landed on the jump board. If the *ephor* raised another black flag, the jump was a foul and would not count. Polydoros was willing the *ephor* to raise a white flag. There was a huge cry from the whole of **Paides Nikandros** when the *ephor* raised the white flag. They all rushed forward to congratulate Polydoros and they threw their arms around him. Polydoros was in the lead with only one competitor to go.

This competitor was the boy from **Paides Nabis** who had been in the lead. Lysander could see that he was clearly nervous. It took him a long time to steady himself and begin his run. He ran a little hesitantly but he took off with a big burst of energy. His jump was big. Polydoros was sure that it was either the same distance as his jump or even a little further. He was no longer sure that he was going to win. There was a long deliberation. The *ephor* looked closely at the board where the boy had started his jump and closely at the point where he had landed. The *ephor* called over another *ephor* and they entered into a long conversation. There was a lot of pointing at the take off board, scratching of heads and checking and double checking of distances. After what seemed an age, during which Lysander thought that his heart was going to explode with the tension, the *ephor* finally raised a white flag. The boy's foot had stayed the right side of the line on the jump board by only a fraction but it was enough. The *ephor* at the other end of the jump announced in a loud voice, "Victory goes to **Paides Nabis**."

Lysander's shoulders sagged with

disappointment. This meant that after the first event, **Paides Nabis** were in the lead. A small flag about the same height as an adult was brought in with an orange background and a large upside down V (which represented the letter L) on it. This was stuck in the ground in front of Nabis's pack. The section of the crowd behind **Paides Nabis** started to shout and cheer loudly to signal their support.

Lysander hung his head in disappointment. Polydoros was one of the boys he was not certain about but to lose in such a fashion was a bitter blow. Lysander began to worry that all his plans were going to come to nothing and that his pack was going to fail. He had visions of them all being whipped to their deaths at the *diamastigosis*.

After a little while of feeling sorry for himself he shook his head, remembered his father's advice and said to himself under his breath, "Stop it, pull yourself together."

There were eight members of his pack and nine events left. Still time to pull things back, though. But how was he going to get a win for Polydoros? It would have to be in the penultimate event - the *stade*. He remembered that in their early training Polydoros's big long legs had meant he was almost as fast at Ariston. They hadn't really trained Polydoros for the *stade* but perhaps his natural talent would carry him through. That, of course, would mean that

Ariston would need to win at another event. This was getting complicated, Lysander thought to himself.

Helen's event was a more straightforward affair. She recorded the longest jump of all the eight girls after the first round and she got a white flag. This meant that she was in the lead after the first jump. In the second round she got another white flag and slightly increased her distance. She was in the lead after the second round. On the final jump she increased her distance still further and none of the other girls came close to her jump. As soon as she saw the white flag raised she knew she had won, even though there were some girls left to jump. When Helen was proclaimed the winner she decided to celebrate by doing a little *bibasis* jump. She leaped as high as she could and slapped her heels against her buttocks as loudly as she could. She shot a glance up to where Gorga and Cleitogora were sitting and she noted that Cleitogora leaned across and whispered something into Gorga's ear. This pleased her. What did not please her, however, was that she did not get a flag placed in front of her like the boys had done. She also noted that the shouts of the crowd were not as loud for her event as they had been for the boy's event.

CHAPTER VIII
The dolichos

The next event was the dolichos, the middle distance race. Lysander felt as confident as he could about this event. The result of the long jump had dented his confidence though and so he was nervous about the outcome. He knew that Leon was one of the best middle and long distance racers he had ever seen but he had not seen any of the other boys run yet and so he couldn't discount the possibility that there might be someone faster than Leon. He was desperate for Leon to win and for his pack to get their first victory. He thought of Apollo and gave a little prayer to him for victory.

Gorga was also confident that Helen would do well as she had already seen her performance as a racer. Gorga's confidence was well founded and, in the end, it turned out that Lysander had nothing to worry about either.

Leon and Helen won their races easily. No-one came close to either of them and they both took an easy victory. Lysander permitted himself a huge sigh of relief. His plan had finally started to work. His team were now equal to **Paides Nabis** and Leon was safe from the *diamastigosis*. One down, seven to go.

Helen was also pleased with herself. She was

in the lead by two events and no-one looked like they could come close to beating her... so far. She knew the fighting and strength events were to come but she could not have made a better start.

CHAPTER IX
Boxing

Next was boxing. Even though Gorga and Helen's mother had told her that girls do not often do boxing the *ephors* had decided to include it in the programme for these games. So, the girls were allowed to compete in this event if they wanted to. Given Helen's earlier experience with Gorga and her nose, she decided against competing. In fact, only four girls took part and the winner was quickly found. It was the girl who had been staring intently at the start of the competition. The score was now 2-1 to Helen.

It was a little different for the boys' event. Lysander nominated Pausarius, Leobotas and Charillos for this event. Leobotas was the best among them and he had trained the longest and the hardest. Charillos lost his first round match and he was quickly out of the competition. Lysander had only put him forward because he was a big boy and he thought that Charillos might be able to absorb a lot of punishment. He hadn't really expected him to win and was slightly relieved that Charillos went out so early as it meant he could save his energy for the shot put - his best event.

Pausarius got through to the second round but he then lost his match to the really big boy from **Paides Dienakes**. It was clear, as Lysander had suspected, that this boy was big and strong and that he was going to make a formidable opponent. Indeed, it was no surprise when the final of the boxing competition was between the big boy from **Paides Dienakes** and Leobotas. It was a tough match. One of the toughest that Leobotas had ever experienced and he had experienced many. He was slightly faster than the big boy and so he managed to land more punches but the other boy just seemed to shrug them off. Every time Leobotas's fist went into the other boy's belly it felt like he had punched a brick wall. By the same token, when the boy landed a punch on Leobotas it felt like he had been hit by a sledgehammer. Leobotas realised that he could not keep this up. If he kept trading punches like this he was going to lose because the other boy was just too big and too strong. He began to doubt in his own mind that he could win and he began to contemplate defeat.

At the end of each round, there was a short pause for the boys to have a little rest and to take some water. During the second break Lysander came over to where Leobotas was sitting. He whispered to him, "Leobotas, you have to use your speed to your advantage. Let the other boy try to hit you but use your speed to dodge and weave out of the way so that he does not land a punch on you. If you let him do that for the next two rounds he will begin to get tired. Then in the last round you can use your speed to hit him as many times as you can... and aim for his head, not his body."

Leobotas nodded. He understood this plan and he put it into action perfectly. He held back. He let the other boy take all the shots and he just dodged or moved out of the way of them. The other boy became more and more frustrated that he couldn't land a blow and he started to try and punch faster so as to catch Leobotas off guard. But, it was no good. Leobotas was faster than him and he continued to dodge. By the fifth and final round it became clear that the other boy was tiring. His cheeks were red and his swings were becoming less frequent and heavier. It was at this moment that Leobotas put into action the second part of Lysander's plan. The other boy made a particularly clumsy effort to yet again land a punch. Leobotas stepped to his left and jabbed a whole series of quick but deadly blows into the side of the boy's head. The boy looked visibly shocked and hurt. He took a step back and shook his head so as to clear it. He shot a glance to the *ephor* as much as to say, "this boy isn't fighting fairly" but the *ephor* paid no attention to him. Before he could do anything else Leobotas had taken a step forward and four more short punches were jabbed into his head. He reeled back again. This time clearly in pain. When Leobotas took another step forward and gave him four more punches to the head the match was all over. The boy fell to his knees and did not stand up. Leobotas was announced as the winner and Lysander's pack received their second flag. Lysander noted to himself with pleasure that his pack were now doing better than **Paides Nabis** and that Leobotas was also now safe from the *diamastigosis*. So far, so good.

CHAPTER X
The javelin

The next event was the javelin. For the girls, only the races and the long jump were compulsory. For all the rest of the disciplines the girls were allowed to choose whether they would compete or not. Helen decided that she would give the javelin a try. She remembered that her brother and his friend had thrown it a little in their garden when they were younger and she had tried it out a few times. She had persuaded Gorga to let her practise it and she felt confident that she would be able to do well. This proved to be a good decision on Helen's part. Only four other girls chose the javelin and it quickly became clear that none of them had practised it much or had any skill.

Helen knew there was a technique to throwing it properly and she put that into practice. She was not brilliant at it but she was definitely better than all the other girls. She was able to throw it without stepping over the throwing line (so she didn't get a black flag) and she was able to make it stick into the ground at the other end. Her distances were not brilliant but she easily won the event. She now had three victories to her score.

Lysander chose himself as the favourite for

this event. As he picked up the javelin he felt the weight of expectation. He had practised hard for this moment and really wanted to succeed in front of his parents and the rest of his pack. He knew that he was showing himself to be a good leader but he knew that he needed to show that, as well as being a leader, he could become a good warrior. He also knew that this event was his own best chance at avoiding the *diamastigosis*.

Lysander was so anxious to succeed that he put all his might into the throw. It went a great distance and he felt that this should be a good score but when he turned around he saw the black flag raised - he had overstepped the throwing line. He held his head in frustration and shame. He heard his father shout something from the crowd but he couldn't make out the words against the noise of the rest of the crowd.

After the first round, a boy from **Paides Nabis** was in the lead. Lysander began to doubt himself. He wasn't sure if he had it in him. He felt that he was going to fail and started to break out into a sweat. He began to have visions of himself in the *limnaeon* being beaten to death with sticks by the rest of his pack. There was a strong vision of Leobotas's face in particular, screwed up tightly with hate - just like he had seen it at the start of their training.

Leobotas must have seen something of Lysander's inner turmoil because he came over and spoke to him. "Come on, Lysander," he said.

"You are the best javelin thrower amongst all of us. You are also a better leader than me and you are the best Spartan boy here. Show everyone what you can do."

Lysander was touched by these words. Leobotas had gone from being a bully and someone who hated him to being someone who was supportive and was giving him compliments. Leobotas's words had an immediate effect. They calmed Lysander down so that his heart stopped beating so fast and they gave him the mental strength to concentrate on what he needed to do.

This time he stepped up to the throwing line with confidence and a spring in his step. Imagining a point in the distance where he wanted the javelin to land he recalled the Athenian doll he used to throw at exactly that spot.

Lysander ran up, used his back and shoulder to impart extra momentum to the javelin and watched with satisfaction as it spun through the air and landed on the spot where he had imagined the dummy. He twisted around quickly to see the *ephor* raise a white flag. The throw counted and it was a huge one.

In fact, there was little need for a third throw. It was clear that none of the other boys were going to get close. So, it was only a matter of time before Lysander was declared the winner. He noted to himself with some satisfaction that both he and his sister had won the javelin. He wanted to go over and give her a hug but he knew that would be forbidden.

Lysander's team now had three victory flags out of four events and **Paides Nabis** had only one. Lysander began to wonder if they might actually win the games after all. He had secretly hoped they might but he hadn't expected that there might be a possibility of that actually happening. **Paides Nabis** had proved themselves to be good opponents but they were not as powerful as Lysander had expected after Nabis had been chosen to be the reader. His pack were building up a good lead over them and it was nearly the halfway point in the games. He also noticed with a little smile to himself that his vision of being beaten at the *diamastigosis* was not going to come true. He laughed at his own silliness and realised that he had again broken his father's third rule - he had felt self-pity.

CHAPTER XI
The shot put

The next event was the shot put. Helen had not practised this event and she decided not to compete. The event was won by the same girl who had won the boxing and so she was now on two victories - only one behind Helen, who saw a pattern emerging. Helen was light, fast and springy. She was winning all the events where these qualities were needed. The other girl was strong and tough. She was winning the events in which these qualities were an advantage. Helen could sense that the competition for the overall winner was shaping up to be a competition between her and this other girl.

For the boys' event Lysander chose himself, Pausarius and Charillos. He was hoping that this would be the event that would see Charillos safe from the *diamastigosis* and would put **Paides Nikandros** too far out in front to be caught.

Charillos was strong but he was also uncoordinated and a bit clumsy. He often found a way to trip up at the last minute, to drop something or generally find some way to come last. Lysander tried to put these doubts to one side. He reminded himself that there was something about the shot put that suited Charillos. It was quite a simple technique and relied mainly on brute strength. He also noted that the big boy from **Paides Dienakes** was not competing. He was still recovering after his defeat to Leobotas in the boxing. Given his size and strength, Lysander had been worried that he would be the obvious boy to win the shot put. The gods seemed to be helping his pack and he felt that the path was now clear for Charillos to win this event.

Lysander made a special point of taking Charillos to one side to speak to him.

"Charillos, this is your big chance," he said. "You have an opportunity to show the whole of Sparta what you can do. I know that you are the best shot putter here. No other boy is as strong as you. Just make sure that you take things slow, get your half spin right and release at the right moment. Remember, whatever you do, don't fall over the throwing line."

Charillos nodded to Lysander and gave him a huge smile.

"Don't worry, Lysander," he said. "You can rely on me."

But the competition was close. Although the big boy from **Paides Dienakes** was not competing there was another boy from **Paides Nabis** who turned out to be incredibly good at the shot put. He looked a little bit like Polydoros in size and frame and Lysander began to wonder if he had made a mistake by not entering Polydoros into this event instead of himself.

The Nabis boy was in the lead after his last throw. There was only Charillos to throw. Lysander took him to one side again.

"Come on Charillos," he said. "This is it. If you win I will make sure that you get an extra portion of honey tonight."

This was all the encouragement that Charillos needed. He stepped up to the throwing line. He was excited. His hands were sweating and his heart was pounding. He seemed to have a heightened sense of all the smells and sounds around him and it was making him a little confused. He realised that his hands were so sweaty that he was going to drop the shot put.

He paused. He bent down. He put the shot put to one side. He picked up some sand and dirt and rubbed it into his hands so that it soaked up some of the sweat and left little grains of sand on his fingers that helped his grip when he picked the shot put up again.

Standing further back from the throwing line allowed him to get a good half spin in. He took half a step even further back and started his spin. In fact, he got so carried away that instead of a half spin he did almost two spins before he released the shot put. This was not an illegal move but it was highly unusual because it could make the thrower dizzy.

Charillos actually released the shot put at the perfect time and it sailed out of his hand. It thumped into the sand a good two fingers further on than the **Paides Nabis** boy's throw. So far, so good. Lysander jumped for joy.

The problem, however, wasn't with the throw - it was at the throwing line. Charillos had indeed made himself dizzy and although he had released the shot put behind the throwing line he was still staggering about and was very close to stepping over the throwing line. If any part of his body stepped over that line before he could steady himself then he would get a black flag. Charillos tottered and teetered for what felt like an age. He realised at the last moment with an agonising feeling that he was not going to be able to stop himself falling over and that his fall was going to take him over the line. It was not elegant and it was not pretty. In fact, many of the audience and the other competitors were laughing out loud and pointing at Charillos. He buried his head in the sand with shame as the *ephor* raised a black flag. Lysander punched the air in front of him with frustration and disappointment. This meant that **Paides Nabis** had a second victory and were only one flag behind Lysander's pack. It also meant that Charillos was not safe from the *diamastigosis*. Lysander was distraught. He now had two team members that were at risk and he couldn't really see how he was going to find a win for Charillos. The shot put really had been his best hope.

I

The end of the shot put marked the half-way point in the competition. The athletic events were an important part of the *gymnopaedia* but they were not the only things planned for the day. The Spartans loved to worship the Gods and the *gymnopaedia* was one of three festivals dedicated to the God Apollo. The half-way point in the competition was when the Spartans chose to dedicate the games to Apollo and to worship him. The religious part of the festival always started with a recital of music. Both Lysander and Helen noticed with interest that the music involved boys and girls who were not much older than them, playing a series of musical pieces. Helen thought to herself that these children must be last year's intake for the *agoge* and so she noted to herself that she and Lysander would probably be providing this entertainment at next year's *gymnopaedia*. The instruments were a mixture of double flutes, hand cymbals and bells. As the girls and boys played these instruments together, one of the boys and one of the girls started to sing some lines of poetry by Tyrtaeus - Sparta's favourite poet. The poem was long but it was about how Apollo favoured the Spartans and about how it was glorious to fight, and if needed, to die for Sparta as a hoplite in the phalanx. At the end of the song, the crowd all stood and cheered. At a signal from the *ephors* they all shouted, "All hail Sparta!" three times in succession.

Next came a dance performed by the *paidiskoi* - Nikandros, Nabis, Dienakes and Agis.

Lysander was surprised to see that Agis had appeared for this section of the festival without his pack. Lysander wondered if this meant that his pack were going to arrive after all - even if a little late. Lysander did not need to worry though. Although Agis had left his pack to lick their wounds he wanted to do his duty and not bring shame on himself. So he had made a point of attending the *pyrrhic* dance, which was set to music and involved the four *paidiskoi* wearing full armour. They each wore a helmet, a large shield, greves which protected their shins and a full size *xyston* or Spartan spear.

The dance involved the teenagers holding their armour and weapons in exaggerated poses for long periods of time. The shield and the *xyston* were heavy - very heavy - and holding them up in the air or away from the body required great strength.

Lysander had felt the weight of such weapons when his father had gifted them to him on his last night at home and he was full of admiration for the *paidiskoi* about how strong they must be to do such moves. Even though the dance lasted for half an hour it felt like only moments for Lysander as he was absorbed in every move. Once again, as soon as the dance had finished the crowd showed their appreciation and shouted, "All hail Sparta!" three times.

Next came a dance by a group of teenage girls. Helen guessed that they were the same age as the *paidiskoi*. She followed the dance carefully and had hoped to see some *bibasis* moves. But there were none. The girls jumped and leaped in rhythmic and athletic moves in time to the music. Once again, at the end of the dance the crowd roared their appreciation in the usual way. As soon as the crowd had finished cheering, the chief *ephor* called the *paidiskoi* girls to the centre arena and declared, "Now we will hear the ridicule songs to mark the end of the half-way point of the games. Show your appreciation for each song and we will judge the winner after all the songs have been heard."

There were four girls and so there were four songs in total. There was one about Charillos and how clumsy he was; there was one about a boy from Nabis's pack; and there was one about the boy from Dienakes's pack who had lost the final of the boxing.

But the song which got the loudest applause of all was the following:

> *When the going gets tough,*
> *are Agis's pack strong enough?*
> *No. They stayed in their beds.*
> *With blurry eyes and sleepy heads.*

Is Sparta safe, when the Persians come?
No. If Agis's pack are to be our walls,
then Sparta is doomed and everything falls.

The chief *ephor* announced this song to be the winner and that Agis's pack would be publicly punished in the agora.

Agis hung his head in shame. Eventually, with tears in his eyes, he stood up and made a plea directly to the chief *ephor*. "My pack has brought great shame on Sparta and the *agoge* today. It is right and just that they should be punished. I am their *paidiskoi* and so I must bear responsibility for their shame. I ask that you either let me administer their punishment or that you include me in it. I will not spare them the rod but if you choose to punish me also then you should beat me the hardest of all."

The chief *ephor* paused for a moment.

"Very well then Agis. You shall receive the same punishment as the rest of the pack. This will absolve you of some of their shame."

There was a lot of noise among the crowd. People generally seemed to think that Agis had acted with honour in asking to be punished along with his pack and there was much discussion about it. Eventually, however, the noise subsided and the *ephor* announced the beginning of the second half of the athletics competition.

CHAPTER XII
Wrestling

Helen was not sure what to do about the wrestling. She did not want the girl with two victories to catch her but the event was wrestling and she was not good at the strength events. She was better suited to running and jumping and she had not practised wrestling. In the end, she decided not to compete and to save herself. She was lucky because the girl who had two wins got to the final of the wrestling tournament and almost won. Fortunately, for Helen the other girl slipped as she was coming in for a final hold and her opponent was able to jump on top of her and pin her shoulders to the ground. The other girl was furious as she was clearly the stronger wrestler but this one mistake had cost her the opportunity to get a third win and she remained on two - one behind Helen.

Lysander put Pausarius forward for this event as his best wrestler. Leobotas was also a strong combatant but he had already won and he didn't want Leobotas to undermine Pausarius's chances. So, instead he chose Polydoros and Teleklos. He didn't expect either of them to do well and he really wanted Pausarius to win. Leobotas protested at being missed out because he thought he had a chance for another victory but Lysander calmed him by explaining that he wanted him to save himself for the pankration and the discus. Leobotas thought about this for a little while and agreed in the end.

To win a wrestling match you had to pin both of your opponent's shoulder blades to the ground at the same time for three seconds. To be good at wrestling required both strength and agility.

Lysander's predictions were right. Both Teleklos and Polydoros went out in the first round and so Pausarius was soon left as the only hope of **Paides Nikandros**.

There was one small problem though. In losing his fight, Teleklos damaged his shoulder a little. His opponent had twisted him into a really exaggerated position and had pushed down on him so hard that he heard something pop in his shoulder. When the hold had been released and he had tried to ease out the pain in his shoulder by moving it he found that it was sore to do so. Lysander was concerned by this development. It meant that Teleklos might not be able to take part in the discus and so his only chance of victory would be in the races.

Lysander did not have much time to worry about this though. Pausarius was continuing to wrestle and he had soon made his way to the final. In fact, the final turned out to be a repeat of the boxing final. It was the same big boy that Leobotas had found himself up against in the boxing that stood in front of Pausarius in the wrestling. Both Lysander and Pausarius knew this was going to be a close match. The other boy was big and strong and, if he got Pausarius in a hold, Pausarius would find it difficult or even impossible to break out of it. Pausarius's only hope was to keep moving and stay light and supple to avoid the big boy getting a firm grip on him.

Lysander called over one of the *helots*.

"Bring me some tincture and some olive oil," he ordered. "This boy needs patching up before he goes in the ring."

The *helot* did as he was told and Lysander started to apply the tincture to the cuts on Pausarius's face. This was allowed and was within the rules. It was not permitted to apply tincture or olive oil to the body for a wrestling match as it made the body too slippery. Once Lysander had finished applying the tincture to Pausarius's face he pretended to wash it off his own hands using the olive oil. In reality he was getting his own hands nice and slippery and covered in olive oil. Just as Pausarius was about to get into the ring he gave him a huge slap on the back and wished him luck in a loud voice.

Lysander managed, in just that simple motion, to get quite a lot of olive oil on Pausarius's back and he knew that this would quickly spread once it mixed with Pausarius's sweat. It did the trick. The oil slowly ran down

Pausarius's back and started to spread over it. Every time the big boy got a firm hold on Pausarius he couldn't maintain it long enough to be declared the victor as Pausarius managed to wriggle and slip his way out of the hold. This happened six or seven times and eventually it started to have the same effect that had happened during the boxing match. The big boy became more and more frustrated. He cursed under his breath that Pausarius was, "As slippery as a greased pig," and that he should, "Hold still so I can squeeze the life out of you."

But this didn't work. Pausarius kept wriggling his way out of the holds. He tried applying his own a few times but the bigger boy was just too strong for him to maintain them. Lysander began to think that this match might be lost when something happened to change the nature of the whole event.

On the seventh attempt to hold Pausarius to the ground, Pausarius managed to slip out of the hold again. The big boy became so frustrated that he swung a punch at Pausarius. It landed square on the side of Pausarius's head and knocked him out cold. He instantly went down like a sack of barley and didn't move for quite a long time until he regained consciousness. The problem for the bigger boy, however, was that this was not a boxing match. It was a wrestling match and it was illegal to throw a punch during a wrestling match. As a result, the *ephor* stepped in and declared Pausarius was the winner because the bigger boy was disqualified. This was another victory flag for Lysander's team. They now had four flags and **Paides Nabis** had only two flags. Lysander was glad that his pack had a two point lead again. This victory did feel a little odd though as Pausarius was still unconscious when it was awarded to the team. Nonetheless, Lysander noted that Pausarius was now also safe from the *diamastigosis*. His plan was still working up to a point.

CHAPTER XIII
Pankration

The next event was the Pankration. It wasn't possible for Helen to fight in the pankration. It was considered such a vicious sport that this event was reserved only for the boys.

In Greek the word pankration roughly means total war. It is a way of fighting that involves a combination of boxing, wrestling and kicking. Other moves are also allowed such as holds, joint-locks and chokes on the ground.

In the rest of Greece there were only two rules - no biting and no eye gouging. In Sparta, there were no rules whatsoever. Anything was possible. The contest was won when one opponent either gave in by raising his index finger to the sky in submission or passed out due to a choke hold. It was a truly vicious sport but Spartan warriors often used it to fight in combat if they lost their *xyston* or their sword.

Leobotas was a natural street brawler of the kind that suited the pankration. He was a bit of a bully and he loved to fight. He also fought dirty, so the pankration suited him to the ground. Lysander had no hesitation in picking him.

The only question was who else to put forward. Even though Ariston was not very good at fighting he put himself forward because he wanted to show Lysander that he had the heart and spirit of a warrior. Lysander accepted his request. His final choice was Charillos. This was not because Charillos was a good fighter. It was because he was big and, as with the boxing, could take a lot of punishment before he gave in.

So, the competition began. Charillos went out in the first round. Ariston managed to win his first match as did Leobotas. In the second round Ariston lost to the big strong boy from **Paides Dienakes** that had fought in both the boxing and the wrestling competition. This boy obviously loved the fighting sports. In fact, the final ended up again being between Leobotas and this boy. As they entered the ring, Leobotas snarled just loud enough so that only the other boy could hear it, "I'm going to beat you again and I'm going to knock you out for knocking out my friend."

The big boy smiled nervously but did not seem to be too intimidated. His confidence did drop a little though as soon as he saw Leobotas take his stance. Leobotas was a natural pankration fighter and immediately adopted the classic pankration stance. This was halfway between the wrestler's frontal pose and the boxer's more sideways position.

Leobotas held both hands high so that the tips of his fingers were just below the top of his head. His front arm was nearly fully extended but not entirely so. Leobotas's back was slightly rounded and his body was slightly leaning forward. The overall effect of Leobotas's stance was to give the impression of a mountain lion, coiled and ready to spring.

The other fighter tried to copy this stance as best he could but he did not look as impressive as Leobotas. As the *ephor* signalled for the match to begin, Leobotas immediately shifted his weight onto his back foot and let loose a vicious kick into his opponent's belly. His groan could be heard all around the stadium. Leobotas followed this up with a grab. He meant to get the boy's ear but he missed and got a handful of short hair. He pulled hard at the hair and it came away from the boy's head with a scream.

The boy put his hands up to his head where his hair had been torn out and Leobotas used this as an opportunity to rain down a series of punches and kicks on his body.

The big boy was tired - he had fought in the final of two competitions already - and was in pain. He couldn't sustain this punishment for long and he quickly fell to his knees. This is what Leobotas had been waiting for. As soon as the boy was on his knees he moved quickly behind him and grabbed one of his arms. He twisted the arm sideways and put it into the air so that the boy's other arm had to touch the ground in order to balance him and stop him from falling over completely. Leobotas put the raised arm into a tight hold, gripping him at the forearm and the wrist. He wrapped both his legs around the shoulder of the boy's other arm.

Leobotas felt sure that the boy could not sustain this hold for long and that he would submit with his index finger. But Leobotas underestimated his opponent. Even though the boy was tired and hurt he was a big strong lad and he had reserves of strength left in him. Using his knee on the ground as a pivot he twisted his body around so that his arm was no longer in the hold and then he bent forward at his waist and used Leobotas's own weight to throw him over his back. Leobotas landed in front of him with a thud. Most of Leobotas's body was now on the ground. Only his head and his shoulders were off it. The big boy then grabbed his head around the throat and proceeded to put a tight choke hold on Leobotas. Leobotas was totally taken by surprise. The big boy had turned the tables on him and he knew he was now in trouble. He squirmed, punched and wriggled but he couldn't loosen the boy's grip on his throat. There was no way out of the snake-like grip he had on him. Leobotas started to feel his breath getting short and realised that the boy was choking him. It would be only a matter of time before he passed out and the contest would be lost. He searched around him frantically with his hands for something to help him. Either a stone or some vulnerable part of the boy's body that he could gouge. The boy was on one knee and the only part of his body that Leobotas could reach from this position was the other boy's foot.

Leobotas could feel the life slowly ebbing from him and he knew that he had only a short time before he would pass out. In a last desperate attempt to get out of this hold he grabbed one of the boy's toes and pulled at it with all his might. He pulled it upwards and backwards as hard and as far as he could. He remembered thinking to himself that he heard a crack like the sound the reed stems had made when they were collecting their bedding. He also remembered that this was his last memory. He wasn't aware of the gasps of horror and delight that came from the crowd. He didn't hear the loud scream of the other boy and he didn't see him raise his index finger to the sky. He didn't see or hear these things because at that point he fainted through lack of air. Just a few moments longer and he would have died.

Revived by having water thrown onto his face, he was slightly stunned and amazed to discover that Lysander was hugging him and shouting.

"You won, you won. I've never seen anything like it in my life. Unbelievable, Leobotas, you are a true champion!"

The level of noise from the crowd was phenomenal. Everyone agreed they had never seen a contest like it and such a contest would have been worthy of the Olympic Games themselves. There was a large roar as the victory banner was brought in and put in front of Lysander's team.

CHAPTER XIV
Discus

That left only three events: the discus, the *diaulos* and the *stade*. Lysander had four of his pack: Polydoros, Charillos, Ariston and Teleklos - who had not won an event and so were still at risk from the *diamastigosis*.

The *diaulos* was a long distance running race and Lysander was confident that Leon would win again. No one had come close to him in the *dolichos* and the *diaulos* was an even longer race and therefore even more suited to Leon's skills.

In training it had been Leobotas who had done the best at discus and they had concentrated on using him in the competition. However, it was clear that after his pankration final there was no way that Leobotas was going to take part in any more events. He was still dazed and coughing from being choked.

So that meant that there was only the discus and the *stade* left from which to fashion a victory for two of the four pack members who had yet to win. Lysander thought carefully about who to put forward. He decided it must be Polydoros, Teleklos and Charillos. He was going to save Ariston for the *stade*. One of these three was going to have to win the discus. He spoke to them all in turn.

"We need three athletes for the discus. Polydoros, what about you? You are strong and you might have a chance."

Polydoros looked a little uncertain but nodded his agreement.

"Good," replied Lysander. "Charillos, what about you? You are excellent at the shot put. The discus is not that much different. Do you think you can give it a try?"

Charillos thought about it carefully and nodded his head in agreement.

"I will try my best. I get confused with the spinning but I am determined to make amends for my failure in the shot put."

"Good," replied Lysander. "Teleklos, what about you?"

Teleklos slowly shook his head. He put his hands up to his shoulder.

"I don't think I can Lysander. My shoulder still hurts from the wrestling. I am not sure I can give it my best and I don't want to let the pack down."

Lysander quickly shook his head. He motioned to Teleklos to move to one side so that he could speak to him privately.

"I know your shoulder is injured a little but I need you to win this competition. I cannot explain to you why because I am sworn to secrecy but there is a special reason why each of you must succeed at an event today. I want Ariston to run in the *stade* and I want you to win the discus. As I told you before I think you will be one of our finest warriors. You just need a chance to prove yourself. This is your chance. Will you trust me on this? Can you do that?"

Teleklos thought about this carefully. There was only a moment's hesitation. Teleklos's face broke into a smile and he replied, "I would be honoured. I consider you my friend as well as my leader Lysander and if you think it is for the best then I have no reason to doubt you."

So, that was settled. The line up for **Paides Nikandros** for the discus would be Polydoros, Teleklos and Charillos. Lysander handed Teleklos a piece of salix bark and said to him, "Here chew on this. It should ease the pain in your shoulder."

Lysander had two more ideas. Firstly, he took Charillos on one side and spoke to him. "Charillos, I have been thinking. You said that you get confused by the spinning turn that is needed in the discus. But the spinning turn is very similar to the one you use for the shot put. It is one-and-a-half turns rather than a half turn. Why don't you use your shot put spin of half a turn and just throw it like that?"

Charillos thought about it carefully.

"I could do," he said, "but it might not go as far if I could do the whole spin."

"I have thought about that too," replied Lysander.

At this point he called Teleklos and Polydoros over as well and spoke to them all.

"The shot put is much heavier than the discus. If you all spend the time from now until you throw the discus by holding a shot put in your throwing arm you will get used to the weight. When you change the shot put for the discus you will instantly feel the difference and the discus will feel a lot lighter as a result. You should be able to throw it further. Those two things together should help you to make a good throw."

All three smiled and nodded. They immediately went over to the shot puts and grabbed hold of one. They spent the remaining time until it was their turn to throw, holding the shot put and getting used to its weight.

Charillos was the first to throw. He switched the shot put for the discus and instantly noticed that Lysander was right. The discus felt as light as a feather in his hand. He could hardly notice its weight in comparison to the shot put. Positioning himself carefully and instead of spinning around one-and-a-half times before throwing, he spun around just half a turn and at the end of his spin he let loose the discus with all his might.

There were a few sniggers from the other packs when they saw Charillos's delivery but their pleasure was short-lived. The discus flew a considerable distance through the air. It was a good throw.

Polydoros was next. Unfortunately, it turned

out that he did not have a gift for this event. Even though he noticed that Lysander was right and the discus felt lighter, he could not get any distance with it.

It was then Teleklos's turn. He did the same as Charillos and switched from the shot put to the discus. He too instantly noticed that it felt light in his hand. Teleklos was also a well coordinated boy. He was fully capable of doing the one-and-a-half spins required before releasing. However, his shoulder was still injured and so he didn't put his full power into the throw. As a result, his discus did not travel as far as Charillos's.

At the end of the first round of throws Charillos was in the lead.

Lysander let out a huge cheer. His plan was working. Charillos was winning. If he could maintain this position then he would be safe from the *diamastagosis*. Lysander was desperate for him to win as he liked Charillos. In the second round Charillos repeated his technique of spinning only half a turn and carrying a shot put around in between. His discus didn't go as far as the first round but it was still the furthest this round. Polydoros had his throw disqualified as he stepped over the throwing line. Teleklos again was unable to put his full effort into the throw and he could not beat Charillos's distance.

As the third round approached Lysander was beginning to feel confident about victory. In the previous one none of the other boys had improved their distances and he was beginning to think that they were all too tired to improve. Charillos might just do this, he thought to himself.

His confidence was soon shattered, however, as one of the boys from **Paides Nabis** started to copy the technique of carrying a shot put about.

It had the desired effect. The boy's throw beat Charillos's first round throw by about the width of a finger. It was not a lot but it was enough to put the Nabis boy in first place. Lysander quickly ran over to Charillos. At this point he didn't mind if either Charillos or Teleklos won. He just wanted his pack to come first to show that they were the best.

"Charillos, it doesn't matter if you come second. But if you want to win you are going to have to do one-and-a-half spins and not just one. You did one-and-a-half when you did the shot put earlier today. You almost got that right. Do you think you can do it again in the discus?"

Charillos gave a big gulp and looked Lysander in the eye.

"I will try," he said.

Charillos stepped up to the throwing line. He stood further back from it so that he could get one-and-a-half spins in. He knew that this amount of quick turns made his head spin and that made him clumsy. He did not want to go over the throwing line as he knew that would get him a black flag and a disqualification.

Nervous about overreaching himself like he did in the shot put, he did his spin incredibly slowly and deliberately. As a result, he gained no extra momentum from the spin and his discus did not travel very far.

Lysander punched the air in front of him with frustration and disappointment. His frustration was compounded when Polydoros also failed in his third throw.

He realised that everything now rested with Teleklos.

Lysander quickly ran over to him.

"Come on, Teleklos," he said. "This is your last chance. You can do it. Remember what I said about the importance of giving it your all. Come on."

Teleklos nodded and gave a gulp.

Swapping his shot put for his discus, he approached the throwing area and steadied himself. Swaying a little from side to side to wind himself up, he then went into his spin. His technique was good and this time he put every ounce of strength that he could muster into the shot. The injury to his shoulder did not prevent him throwing as he had feared but when he used full power the pain intensified. It caused him to take just a little power off his throw. His discus landed close to, but behind the discus of the **Paides Nabis** boy.

Lysander's pack had suffered another defeat.

Paides Nabis were only two flags behind them with two events to go. But worse, much worse, Lysander now realised that at least half of his pack were looking at the possibility that their names would go into the hat for the *diamastigosis*.

Helen was faced with the same dilemma she had had earlier. Should she compete in an event that she knew she couldn't win or should she save herself for the last two running events that she felt she would have the best chance in.

In the end, it was an easy choice. She hadn't trained for the discus and she was not good at strength events. She decided not to compete.

What was bad for Helen though was the fact that the winner of the discus was the girl who had already won two events. This meant that this girl had now won three events and was the joint leader with Helen. Helen desperately wanted to win to show her mother and father that they could be proud of her and her brother and that she was every bit as good as him.

She knew that she must win either the *diaulos* or the *stade*. The *diaulos* was her best chance.

CHAPTER XV
The Stade

Helen was faced with a difficult choice. Should she race in the *stade* as well as the *diaulos* or should she save herself for the *diaulos*?

The girl who was just behind her was big and strong, suited to the fighting and the throwing events. She was not built for running and Helen decided to take a calculated risk. She guessed that the other girl would not win the *stade* and so she decided to save herself for the final race.

It was an inspired decision. Helen's instincts proved correct and the other girl did not win. That honour went to one of the smaller, slimmer girls.

Lysander was worried about the *stade*. He had four pack members who had not won an event and he realised with a heavy heart that he could not save them all. In the circumstances he was keen to ensure that one of them won but he knew in his heart of hearts that Ariston was the better sprinter and he was more likely to win than Teleklos or Polydoros. Charillos was not suited to an event like this and Lysander didn't even give this possibility a second thought.

He knew the line up that he must put forward would be Polydoros, Ariston and Teleklos. He felt that Ariston had a strong chance and possibly Polydoros but he was not completely confident that either had it in them. He also felt that he did not have the words that he needed at this point to give any of his pack the boost they needed. Lysander had had two nights of poor sleep and he felt as though he had used all his energy and his fine words throughout the day. As a result, at this last hurdle he was speechless. He felt like a failure.

The *stade* was a fast race. The athletes threw themselves down the track with all of their speed and the race was over in a very short amount of time. Almost the blinking of an eye. In fact, it was said that if you coughed or sneezed during the *stade* you would miss the action.

As the boys lined up on the start line Lysander noticed that Ariston and Teleklos were side by side. He thought of telling them to separate a little but decided in the end that this was not needed.

The *ephor* shouted, "Go!"

Lysander watched as a blizzard of action took place. He didn't see what happened to cause it but watched with horror as Ariston fell onto the track and then a moment later Teleklos fell on top of Ariston so that they both ended in a heap on the ground.

What he hadn't seen was that the boys from **Paides Nabis** had hatched a plot to ensure that his pack would not win another event. One of the Nabis boys had made sure that he started at the side of Teleklos and when the command of "Go!" had been given, he had deliberately stumbled into the back of Teleklos. Teleklos had gone off fast and so this stumble only caught the back of his heel. That was enough though to trip him forwards and that sent him crashing into the back of Ariston.

So, in less than the twinkling of an eye, three boys were laid out on the track. As Polydoros became aware of this he stopped for a moment to check what was going on and to ensure that they were unharmed. One of the boys from **Paides Dienakes** did the same and stopped to stare at the crash.

The other two boys from **Paides Nabis** did not stop however. They knew perfectly well what had happened as they had helped to plan it and just put their heads down and ran as fast as they could. By the time Polydoros came to his senses and realised what was happening it was too late. He was too far behind and the two Nabis boys came first and second.

Lysander threw up his hands in frustration and turned to the *ephor* for judgement.

"They cheated," he shouted. "They cheated!"

But the Nabis boy who had pretended to fall was now up on his feet and was explaining agitatedly to the *ephor* that it had been an accident and that he was just as upset as everybody else to stumble like that.

The *ephor* listened to all the arguments and

the shouting. After a short while he raised his hands and declared in a loud voice, "The result stands."

Lysander realised with horror that not only could his friend Ariston not avoid the *diamastigosis* now but that **Paides Nabis** was only one flag behind his own pack with just one event to go.

He felt that sense of panic rise up inside him again and started to have visions of them all inside the *Limnaenon*. Then he remembered that the final event was the *diaulos* and that Leon was clearly the best long distance runner among all the boys. He shouldn't have anything to worry about. He let out a sigh of relief.

CHAPTER XVI
The Diaulos
(the girls' race)

Helen was feeling the same. She was confident that she would win this race.

The girl who shared first place with her had other ideas. She had a plan that was designed to stop Helen in her tracks. She left the arena for a few minutes pretending that she needed the toilet. She needed to get to the dirt and gravel that was on the ground at the back of the stadium where the spectators stood. This part of the stadium was not swept like the other areas. There were bits of rubbish and the odd stone mixed into the sand and dirt. The girl dropped to her knees and she carefully selected three stones. These were small stones that she could hide in her hand but which had sharp edges. The kind that would dig into your feet and hurt you. As soon as she had got the three stones she needed she returned to the competition area to get ready for the race.

The *diaulos* for competitors of this age was ten laps of the stadium. It would get longer as the competitors got older but, for the moment, it was ten laps.

The girl knew that Helen was quicker than her over the full distance and would beat her.

So she knew that, in order for her plan to work, she must get out in front of Helen as quickly as possible. And that is exactly what she did. As soon as the race started the other girl sprinted ahead so that she was in the lead. Helen thought this was a bit crazy as no-one could run the whole *diaulos* by running at this speed. Helen decided that she would just settle into her normal pace and expected that she would catch the girl up in no time. And that is what happened. As they approached the end of the first lap Helen had almost caught the other girl, who had visibly slowed down. The rest of the field was a short way behind these two. It was at this point that the other girl released her first stone. She waited until Helen was close to her and then she dropped the stone into the area that she thought Helen's path would take her. The stone missed its mark by a small amount. It actually bounced over Helen's foot and she didn't tread on it. In fact, Helen wasn't even aware of what was happening. She had no idea and just continued to run.

The other girl looked behind her and saw Helen almost on her shoulder and she realised this was her final chance to hobble Helen. She knew she couldn't win but if she could stop Helen winning they would share the prize for first place. So, instead of dropping the remaining stones one by one she decided to release the final two together. This time her strategy worked. One of the stones bobbled underneath Helen's foot and as her foot landed on the track the stone dug its way into her heel. It went in deep and touched the bone. Helen jumped in the air with a huge cry of pain. She pulled up quickly from running and lifted her affected leg to see the stone protruding from her heel. She tried to pull it out quickly but it was in deep and it took her a few moments. She started to run again but discovered it was not as easy as before. As she tried to get back into the race she noticed two things. Firstly, all the other girls had gone past her and were now about half the length of the stadium in front of her. Secondly, it was really painful to put her foot down and she couldn't really run properly. She hobbled a little and then stopped again. She turned to the *ephor* so as to plead with him for the race to be stopped because the other girl had cheated. But the *ephor's* face was unmoved. The track was swept every day but occasionally stones did get missed. It was just bad luck as far as the *ephor* was concerned. Helen should just get on with it. The *ephor* was happy as it meant that he could punish the *helots* later for not sweeping the track properly.

Helen realised there was nothing more to do. She would have to run through the pain if she was to win this final event. She gritted her teeth and tried to imagine herself as being outside her body watching herself suffering the pain of running but without experiencing it directly herself. It worked a little.

Helen was able to get into a running rhythm again. Each step was painful and for a little while she left a bloody foot print in the sand with every stride she took. Helen couldn't help it but she felt the tears well up into her eyes as she tried to force back the pain and rise above it. As she went past one section of the audience all of a sudden she was aware of a loud voice shouting at her, "Come on little flea! You can do it! Remember your run to the Eurotas. Your feet were just as bad then!"

It was Gorga. She was standing up and encouraging Helen at the top of her voice. Helen thought that Gorga thought she was just a silly girl who couldn't take a bit of pain. She had expected Gorga to have harsh words for her at the end. But here she was, encouraging her and urging her on to victory. This support from Gorga was just the help that Helen needed. She bit her lip, wiped the tears from her eyes and reached down into herself to tap into all her reserves of strength and stamina. Slowly, she began to close the gap on the other girls. First she passed one, then she passed another and another. She heard the bell that marked the beginning of the last lap. She had three girls in front of her and only one lap to go.

She had passed the first girl by the first corner. Only two girls to go. The second girl was the one who had cheated by dropping the stone in her path. She had used all her energy at the start and was no longer in front. Helen passed her at the halfway point. She was tempted to trip her or punch her as she went past but she knew that she would get a black flag for that and she didn't want to be disqualified. So, she satisfied herself with simply hissing, "Cheat," as she went past.

The final girl was about ten strides ahead of her and there were about fifty strides to go to get to the line. Helen dug deep inside herself for one last time. She let out an inner roar of frustration which gave her an extra burst of energy. Lunging forward and running at a full sprint she ran so fast that she thought her lungs would burst. Helen never ran like this normally because it was a crazy speed for a long distance race but she knew she had to do this to win. It worked. She passed the final girl just before the finish line and she went over the line first. She had won!

The whole stadium erupted into cheers. The crowd had not seen a girls' race as good as this for some time and they were excited and delighted to see Helen win after having come from so far back and with a foot injury that was still bleeding a little. To win despite being injured was a very Spartan thing to do and was seen as a virtue. Some sections of the crowd began to chant her name. The loudest voice of all was that of Gorga.

Helen hardly had the strength to register

what had happened. She had won the *gymnopaedia* by four events to three. This meant that she was the best overall girl for that year and that, more importantly for her, she had completed Gorga's challenge and would be allowed to try out for the state *bibasis* school. She knew that she should be happy but she was just so drained by her efforts in the *diaulos* that the emotions would not come to her.

She was only vaguely aware of the slight pulling sensation on her chiton until it became more insistent and a voice accompanied it.

"It is me, Pylos, Mistress Helen. Mistress Gorga has asked me to give you this drink to help refresh you. Please drink some now."

And with that he handed a beaker to her that appeared to be filled with various leaves and herbs. She tasted the drink and noticed that it was sweet. She found the taste comforting and she settled back into her chair to finish the drink. Her attention also moved to the final of the boys' race.

CHAPTER XVII
The Diaulos
(the boys' race)

The nine runners from the three packs all took their places on the start line. The *diaulos* was to be ten laps of the arena. Lysander had thought long and hard about which members of his pack should participate. Leon, of course, was an obvious choice. He was a talented long distance runner and Lysander felt that he had a strong chance of winning the race and in so doing he would ensure that **Paides Nikandros** won the overall competition.

The other two places were actually easy choices but, nonetheless, Lysander agonised over them. He wanted to make sure that he had the best possible team and his mind kept running over all the possibilities. He wanted to give the four boys who had not won anything one last chance to prove themselves. However, this was not as easy as he would have liked it to be.

Charillos was clearly not suited to running. He was completely the wrong build to be a runner and it would be a stupid choice to include him. Teleklos could have run but was injured and his fall in the *stade* had made it even worse. Although the injury was to his shoulder it would affect his running as a good running action needed both the arms and the legs moving in unison. Ariston was similarly unsuited to distance running. He was a good sprinter but he had no stamina for the long haul. Besides, his knees were badly scraped from being pushed over in the last race. In the end, Lysander decided to give Polydoros one last chance. He also decided to include himself in the lineup. Annoyed with himself that he hadn't said anything about the line up in the last race he reasoned that at least if he was on the track he could keep an eye out for any further problems. He quickly realised that this had been a wise choice. Lysander spotted with a rising sense of anger that all three of the **Paides Nabis** boys had deliberately chosen to line up close to Leon. They were packing around him tightly and Lysander was in no doubt that they intended to cheat again and take Leon out of the race. He quickly called to Polydoros.

"Polydoros, come with me. They are trying to stop Leon from winning. We must help him."

Polydoros was quick to react. Both he and Lysander moved over to where Leon was and they tried to squeeze in between the Nabis boys so that they couldn't trip Leon like they had done to Ariston.

This pushing and jockeying for position quickly descended into a near fight.

"Don't hit them or push them," shouted Lysander. "We don't want to get disqualified. But don't give any ground."

Polydoros followed these instructions well and the whole line up descended into chaos.

Eventually one of the *ephors* stepped in.

"Boys, stop fighting!" he shouted. "This is a running race. Not a fighting competition. **Paides Nabis**, you line up here. **Paides Dienakes** you go in the middle. **Paides Nikandros** you go at the end here."

In this way, the *ephor* separated the three teams and Lysander had achieved his objective. He had made sure that Leon had a clear path. Just before the *ephor* shouted, "Go!" to start the race, Lysander managed to speak to Leon.

"Leon, they are going to try to trip you or stop you in some way. You must get out in front and not get anywhere close to one of the Nabis boys."

Leon nodded his understanding.

Leon knew what Lysander wanted him to do but he had a technique for running such races that suited him well. He knew how to win a race and he knew what pace he needed to run at to do that. So, he went off at his usual even speed. He knew that if he went too fast too quickly he would tire towards the end and that someone might then pass him.

His normal pace was quite quick but it was not a sprint and so this allowed the Nabis boys to run fast in order to try to crowd around him again. Their plan was to run shoulder to shoulder with him and then slow him down with their own bodies in the way while their third runner overtook Leon and went ahead.

Lysander and Polydoros were by now alive to this possibility and as soon as they spotted the Nabis boys heading for Leon they also moved so that they were shoulder to shoulder with Leon on either side. In that way, they blocked the Nabis boys from getting close to Leon. It took two laps for the Nabis boys to change their strategy.

Leon was quick and Lysander and Polydoros were struggling to keep up with him. It was clear that the two Nabis boys who were supposed to crowd Leon out were not good runners and they couldn't keep up with him either. They were soon half a lap behind.

The only Nabis boy who could keep up was the one who was supposed to overtake Leon once he had been crowded out. This boy came up with a different plan. If he couldn't get past Leon because he had been crowded out then he would resort to tripping Leon, just like they had done with Ariston and Teleklos. He knew that he only had the energy to catch Leon once and so he put his head down and motored as hard as he could to get behind him.

It took Lysander a moment to work out what was happening. He was concentrating on staying by Leon's side so that he couldn't get crowded out. He suddenly became aware of one of the Nabis boys now trying to get behind Leon. He guessed quickly what was happening

THE TALES OF HELEN AND LYSANDER

and shouted to Polydoros, "Quick, Polydoros, we must both drop behind Leon. They are trying to get behind him to trip him."

And so both Polydoros and Lysander shifted their positions and took up guard behind Leon. The Nabis boy was thwarted and Lysander could tell he had been right in his guess as the disappointment on the Nabis boy's face was plain for all to see.

Indeed, **Paides Nabis** seemed to have no options left to them now. No-one could catch Leon and he started to stride out in front. Not even Lysander or Polydoros could keep up with him and he started to build a big lead.

In fact, it was this lead that gave the Nabis boys one last chance to stop Leon. It was on lap six that Leon had built such a big lead that he started to come up behind the two Nabis boys who were now at the back. They were still on their sixth lap but Leon was about to start his seventh lap. If Leon was going to lap them then he would have to pass them. If he was going to pass them then they could trip him. They were jubilant. They thought that they had lost the race and their plan had failed but Leon's own ability was about to present them with another chance to take him out.

Lysander took a few moments to work out what was happening. He was just beginning to think the result of the race was a foregone conclusion when he spotted what was happening. He saw Leon striding out ahead and he could see that at this pace he was going to pass the two Nabis boys in a short while. He knew instinctively that they would try to trip him if he did that. He shouted ahead to Leon, "Leon! Don't pass them until Polydoros and I are with you. Slow down a little."

Leon heard the instruction. Even though he didn't understand why and that it went against his every instinct he trusted Lysander and so followed his advice. He slowed his pace so that he was no longer closing on the Nabis boys.

In the meantime, Lysander and Polydoros slowed their own pace right down so that the Nabis boys began to close on them and were in danger of lapping them. The Nabis boys knew what was happening but there was nothing they could do about it, other than stop in the middle of the track. If they did that though they knew they would be disqualified. And so, in this way, Lysander and Polydoros caught up with the Nabis boys and ran shoulder to shoulder with them. At this point, Lysander shouted over his own shoulder, "Leon, you can go past us now. Go, win the race!"

Leon did not need any more encouragement. He put his head down and he ran like the wind. He passed the clutch of boys that seemed to be jockeying for position without incident and he sped past them.

And that was that. Leon now strode out with

the end in sight and comfortably passed the line in first place a short while afterwards.

Paides Nikandros had won the race! Lysander breathed a huge sigh of relief.

CHAPTER XVIII
The Awards Ceremony

Lysander's pack had won six events and they were clearly the champions for the day. He saw his mother and father in the crowd. They were not hard to find. They were both beaming with pride. They were hugging each other and jumping on the spot with joy. They were chanting both his and Helen's names. He knew that he was not allowed to speak to them but he could wave to them or give them some sign of recognition.

He turned to find Helen and saw her across the other side of the stadium. She was excited. Now recovered, she was jumping for joy and waving to Gorga and Pylos in the crowd. Lysander knew that he should give her a wave and blow her a kiss. But he could do no such thing. His plan to save his entire pack from the *diamastigosis* had been going so well until the final few events. It had all come unstuck at the last minute and Teleklos, his closest friend Ariston, Charillos and Polydoros would all have their names entered into the hat to see if they would undergo the *diamastigosis*. And worse than that Lysander felt that he had failed in his leadership just at the point when it was tested the most. Ariston, Teleklos and Polydoros had needed him to be at his best in those final moments but he had no ideas and nothing to say to them. He felt a strong sense of failure.

Once the excitement in the crowd died down the competition finished with the awards ceremony. The winner of each event was called forth in turn and presented with a laurel wreath, in honour of Apollo, to mark their victory by the chief *ephor*. The wreath, made of branches from a laurel tree, was fashioned into a little crown which was placed on the head of the winner.

Every winning member of Lysander's pack received a laurel wreath. Lysander and Pausarius received one and Leon and Leobotas each received two. There was also a special wreath, which also had little bits of gold thread inserted into it for the leader of the pack with the most victories.

Obviously, this gold wreath was placed on Lysander's head. But he quickly took it off and beckoned to his pack speaking to them quickly but in hushed tones.

"We all deserve to be winners today. You have all made me incredibly proud to be your leader and Leobotas has done a fantastic job as my second in command. I want you all to wear a laurel. Leon and Leobotas will you give one of your laurels each to Teleklos and Ariston? Polydoros and Charillos, I want you to have my gold laurel. Hold it together and hold it aloft with pride."

Without a moment's hesitation the boys all followed these instructions and were soon all wearing or holding a victor's laurel of some kind.

Lysander did this as a sign to the *ephors*. It was his way of sending a message to say to them, "My whole team are winners. Everyone's contribution has been essential. Don't you dare enter their names into the diamastigosis."

Helen received four individual wreaths for each of her victories and she received the golden wreath for winning the most individual events. Both she and Lysander were made to stand in front of the crowd and to receive their applause. This lasted a long time. It felt like forever that they had to stand there. It did mean, however, that she and Lysander could stand close to each other. Helen grabbed his hand half-way through the applause and she raised both their arms together in a victory salute. The crowd roared even louder. Lysander realised that Helen was happy and that he still owed her a huge debt. He turned to her and shouted above the noise of the crowd, "Thank you sister. I wouldn't have been here today without your help. Those boys meant to hurt us."

She smiled back at him and acknowledged his thanks.

I

After all the excitement of the awards ceremony was over Helen and Lysander went back to their respective parts of the stadium. They started to clear away the equipment and the crowd started to filter away back to their houses.

Lysander and Helen thought that it was all over and that was the end of their day. But just at that point, the woman who had been sitting next to Gorga came over to speak to Helen.

"I am Cleitogora," she said. "I wish to speak to you."

Helen looked expectantly at the woman.

"That was an impressive performance today, Helen. I would like you to come and try out for the state *bibasis* school. Come to see me with Gorga early next week."

Helen beamed a huge smile and thanked the woman.

"It will be a huge honour," she said.

At the same time that Helen was speaking to Cleitogora the chief *ephor* came up to Lysander and said, "Lysander, I know you are disappointed that you did not win every event. Nonetheless, you won six events and I wanted you to know that is equal to the record for the number of events won by a *paides* pack at a *gymnopaedia*."

Lysander looked at the chief *ephor* and realised that he was trying to be kind to him. He realised that he was doing him a great honour by talking to him in this way. Lysander smiled at the chief *ephor* and replied, "Thank you. I appreciate the compliment."

He wanted to go on to explain that he was still disappointed because he knew that four of his pack might get nominated for the *diamastigosis*. However, he knew that he wasn't supposed to know about this and so he could not say this. So, he kept quiet.

However, the chief *ephor* had not finished. He continued, "I also want you to know that I am aware that the **Nabis** boys cheated in the sprint race and that they tried to cheat in the last race."

Lysander's pulse quickened. Did this mean that the chief *ephor* was going to change his mind? Was there to be a reprieve for Ariston? The chief *ephor* continued, "I am also aware Lysander that you cheated in the wrestling. I saw you apply the oil to Pausarius's back. I thought that was clever - just what a Spartan should do."

Lysander's face quickly went red. He thought he had got away with this trick unnoticed and that he had been clever. He was shocked to find out the *ephor* had spotted him.

The *ephor* continued, "I also think what the Nabis boys did was clever. Just what a Spartan should do. Spartans need every weapon in war. They need strength, skill and guile. I think you have learned an important lesson about guile in these games."

Lysander looked at the chief *ephor* with shock on his face. He was more clever than Lysander had given him credit for and he could sense that the *ephor* was right. The athletics competition had been a kind of training for war and Lysander had learnt some important lessons about strategy.

"Now go," said the chief *ephor*. "Congratulate your sister. She has done well and brought honour to your family. As have you. Spend a few moments also with your parents. You and they deserve that as a reward for your achievement."

Lysander smiled at him and said, "Thank you."

To be continued…

Helen and Lysander will return in The Tales of Helen and Lysander - Book 2, Growing Pains.

ACKNOWLEDGEMENTS

I should like to record my thanks to the following people: my friend Ben Leyburn who gave me helpful feedback on the early draft of my first chapter. His comment, "Well, it's not rubbish," gave me all the encouragement I needed to carry on. My friend Kurt Janson who gave me helpful feedback on the plot and was supportive throughout. My friend Helen McInnes who gave me invaluable help in finding a publisher. Fellow authors, Martin White (Faze: City of Addicts) and Mike Hollow (The Blitz Detective) who gave me advice on the world of publishing. And, most of all, my wife Sian, who gave me her support and encouragement throughout. I am extremely grateful to all of them.

Final chapter illustration by: Emilia Both-D'Angelo

ALSO FROM TIM SAUNDERS
PUBLICATIONS

Hong Kong by Mary Levycky
The Price of Reputation by Lin Bird
A Lesson in Murder by Lin Bird
Love and Death by Iain Curr
The Fourth Rising Trilogy
by Tom Beardsell
Letters from Chapel Farm
by Mary Buchan
That was now, this is then
by Philip Dawson-Hammond
Healthcare Heroes by Dr
Mark Rickenbach
Shadows and Daisies by Sharon Webster
Lomax at War by Dan Boylan
A Life Worth Living by Mary Cochrane
Faze by MJ White
A Dream of Destiny by DoLoraVi
Dreams Can Come True by
Rebecca Mansell
The Collected Works of TA Saunders

tsaunderspubs.weebly.com

Unsolicited manuscripts accepted

ABOUT THE AUTHOR

Stephen Hodgson

After gaining an MA in Philosophy, Stephen worked as a senior civil servant in Whitehall, London. As his two sons grew up he discovered that one of the nicest things he could do with them was to sit down, open a book and enter a whole new world together. They often transported themselves into the worlds of Middle Earth, Narnia, outer space and a hundred other places. Michael Morpurgo's books were a favourite for them and an inspiration for Stephen - his books deal with historical settings but do not shy away from difficult themes. Stephen's aim is to do the same.

Printed in Great Britain
by Amazon